S0-ASF-302

I Always Get a Great Parking Space!

MARGARET-ANN BOGERTY

RECOGNIZING GOD IN THE ORDINARY BLESSINGS

To the Brasley's — You both are truly blessed and highly favored.

Margaret-Ann
1 Dec 07

PMP POWER MARKETING PUBLISHING COMPANY
ALEXANDRIA/VIRGINIA

I Always Get A Great Parking Space!
Recognizing God in the Ordinary Blessings
Copyright ©2007 by Margaret-Ann Bogerty

Power Marketing Publishing
P. O. Box 15631
Alexandria, VA 22309
(703) 780-2745
powermrktg@aol.com
www.greatparkingspace.com

Photo of author with her mother by Darnley R. Hodge, Jr.
Imagination, Inc., Oxon Hill, MD

Back cover photo of author by Ruth Bogerty-Wright
Cedar Hill, TX

Book design and composition by Eric Bannister
GravityDesigns
gravity_movement@yahoo.com

Printed in the United States of America

ISBN 978-0-9766165-0-4
Library of Congress Cataloging-in-Publication Data
2006940392

This book is dedicated to my mother

CLARA BRONSON BOGERTY

*A wise woman of grace and dignity. Her life-long example of
honorable Christian living influenced not only my life,
but also every thought contained herein.
I love you, Mom!*

Contents

Preface

There was once a very popular TV commercial that asked in a whimsical way a most provocative question, "What do you want on your tombstone?" In days past, a person's name was often based on some perceived characteristic, metaphorical inspiration, or experience occurring at or near the time of birth that defined who the person was or would become. Gravemarkers often reflect some attempt at this. The next time you're in a cemetery, notice the inscription on the memorials you see.

Advertisers are masters at creating metaphors for their products and services by subscribing names and slogans depicting the company's desired perception or service philosophy, such as "The Ultimate Driving Machine" (BMW), "We Got That" (Staples), "We Do Chicken Right" (KFC), and "Have It Your Way" (Burger King).

In the same sense, every human life is descriptively a metaphor. And each is meaningful enough to be described in at least a word or two. Whether your metaphor is subscribed or prescribed, every day presents a new opportunity to define or reinforce your life meaning and to choose your life's outlook.

So, answer the question: "What *do* you want on your tombstone?" Think long and hard about it. Summarize in a word or two *who* you are and *what* you believe, in whatever way that is true and whatever is you. Create a word-picture of yourself and title it any way you wish—"God's Favorite Child," "Ah, No Problem," "Murphy's Law Personified." You can decide for yourself what word or phrase best suits your life or the life you want. Your metaphor can serve to remind you of your core beliefs and, if it's positive, inspire you to go on in a positive way.

I Always Get A Great Parking Space! is my life metaphor and personal affirmation of the fact that life is a wonderful thing. To have life on whatever the terms is the greatest gift possible. The feeling of elation and gratitude I experience when I literally find a great parking space may seem a little bit odd, but it goes to the heart of who I am and what I believe. Consider it my take on life: symbolic of my positive outlook in general. Finding a parking space in the perfect location, especially when the odds are terribly against me, conjures up a pleasant picture and an exhilarating state of mind. I always feel great when I get one, and I try to duplicate the feeling in other ways with every passing day.

I Always Get A Great Parking Space! not only identifies me, but it is a coping mechanism that fuels my outlook of positive expectation whenever a boost of encouragement is needed; when I'm faced with overwhelming challenge or a situation I cannot change . . . and that can be often! It is my revised perspective on the incredible privilege we have as children of the King to throw ourselves completely into His loving care and embrace hope every day. And, it is my humble attempt to share the joy I've come to expect living through my personal relationship with Jesus Christ, my Savior, Lord, and Friend.

Throughout this book, the one thing I've tried to be is honest. I wanted you to know that the thoughts and ideas it contains come from someone who can genuinely relate to difficulty and challenge. The experiences I've written about are all personal and real. Of course, many of the names have been changed for reasons of privacy.

In my life there have been times I've been worried out of my mind not knowing what the outcome of a frightening situation would be; uncertain as to whether the Lord would come through for me "this" time . . . or was he sick of me, and had had enough of my shenanigans. *Hey, I'm human!* During those times, I didn't have any answers. All I could see was this train speeding towards me as I lay helplessly tied to the proverbial railroad tracks. Yet . . .

I'M STILL HERE!

And when I look back over my life, there's never been even one need He's overlooked, even though from wherel stood the situation was so dark I could hardly see my hand before my face. But

GOD IS A MERCIFUL GOD.

". . . the darkness and the light are both alike to [Him]" (Psalm 139: 12)! Only by His inexhaustible Grace are any of us here!

I pray that you allow the peace that I've come to know through Christ to accompany the promises of His faithful provisions in all things to rule your thoughts day by day. Trust Him. Submit and obey Him. Expect today to be blessed and you will discover, as I have, all the wonderful "great parking spaces" He has reserved for you in the parking lot of life no matter what you may be facing.

**God's record is 100%.
He hasn't failed me yet . . .
and He won't fail you either!**

Calvary was the ultimate expression of His commitment to take care of us in *every* way we need to be taken care of. And, that includes when it's only a matter of finding a place to park the car!

Be encouraged. It's already all right!

MAB
Alexandria, Virginia

Acknowledgments

From conception to inception to fulfillment, were it not for the overwhelming love, encouragement, and support of a lot of people who believed in me, and who believed in what I had to say, the ink would have never been put to paper.

First, I give thanks, honor, and praise to My Lord and Savior, Jesus Christ, who by the power of His Holy Spirit, enabled me with the insight and tenacity to see this work through.

Furthermore, I thank and praise Him for the gift of a wise and prayerful mother, who is undoubtedly the single-most important distinction between the person I am and the person I could've been were it not for her. Her deep trust in the Lord underscores a model of integrity and high personal standards exhibited throughout her life. Nothing I say could ever adequately express the depth of my love and respect for you Mom. You are a blessing beyond measure. And, you have my humblest gratitude.

To the greatest kids on earth, Beverly and Darnley, there are no words to express how much you mean to me and how much I treasure the wonderful life I've enjoyed with you. If I had ever a doubt as to whether or not the Lord loves me, I've but to look in those sparkling eyes for therein lies all the assurance I'll ever need. You are my greatest pride and joy. I'm so grateful and divinely privileged to be the one you call "Mom." Thanks, Nerds! I love you! You're the absolute best!

To my one and only brother, Sidney Bronson, and sisters Kathleen Johnson Walker, Lula Mae Bogerty, Irene Bogerty Lowry, Ruth Bogerty-Wright, and Denise Bogerty-Bryant, when have you ever not been there for me? There has been no one more lavish in faith, support, and encouragement than all of you. Your friendship, honesty, and humor have been the mainstay of my life. Thank you for years of love and incessant laughter. The absence of either of you from my life would be a loss on a magnitude too deep to contemplate. I love you from the deepest caverns of my heart.

Many thanks go out to my dear friends and spiritual mentors, Elder Joseph A. Robinson, Pastor and Founder of the Royal Oak Pentecostal Church in Landover, Maryland, and his wife, co-founder Evangelist Julia Robinson, whose friendship and love bonded us the first day we met almost twenty years ago. Thank you for believing in me and for keeping me reminded of the special work the Lord has for me to do.

I'd like to thank Pastor David Rhodenhizer and the members of Calvary Road Baptist Church in Alexandria, Virginia for welcoming me so warmly and so sincerely. A special thanks to all the ladies in Rowena Haley's Grace Bible Class for extending such tremendous and much-needed love and spiritual support.

Much thanks is extended to Helena Douglas, Senior Director, Clemson University Office of Off-Campus, Distance, and Continuing Education, and sponsor of the Professional Development for Women Conferences, Laurie Haughey, and Carol Richardson for providing the microphone and platform that enabled me to first test the veracity of the contents of this book on audiences around the country.

To Attorney John Wesley Davis, the most authentic individual I have ever known. Thanks for always making my family and me feel special. You'll always be special to us, too.

To my buddy, Mark Cummings whose love, encouragement, and humor have for more than eighteen years helped me through the most challenging times. Thank you for standing with me.

Thanks to my friend, James "Jay" Griffin of Rialto, California, whose insight more than twenty-two years ago disclosed qualities and potential in me I hadn't yet realized myself.

To Chris Francone and Sandy McNeil whose eternal perspective and love of life continuously inspire me. And, thanks to my dear friend Roland Ezike whom I'm sure God put here to love me and to take care of my car (smile!). Much love to everyone in the Alexandria/Mount Vernon Office of Weichert Realtors. I love you guys. To my dear friends Lloyd and Delena Jones of Arlington, Texas, thank you for giving me the courage to take this project on. Your guidance and confidence is surely what put me over the edge.

To my book designer and friend Eric Bannister, "thanks" is hardly adequate to express my appreciation for your incredible patience and for the caring way you embraced this work which could not have been completed without you. And finally, thanks to Cliff Johns for his editorial assistance and encouragement of the work.

Wherefore, if God so takes care of the grass of the field which today is, and tomorrow is cast into the oven, shall he not much more [take care] of you, Oh ye of little faith?

Matthew 6:30

TRUST AND FAITH

CHPTR1

♥ STATE OF JOY ♥

I Always Get a Great Parking Space!

It's true. I surely do. It doesn't matter how crowded the lot is or how many other cars I'm competing with. No matter how unlikely it may seem, I *always* get a great parking space.

Let me illustrate:

Several years ago, I attended the Christmas party of a company I had been soliciting as a client. It was held at the most prestigious officers' club on one of the military installations in the Washington, D.C. area. Never wanting to be the first at such an event for fear of appearing overly anxious, I left home in time to arrive fashionably late (about a half hour or so after the party had started).

Once cleared by the officer at the gate, I drove on into the guest parking lot to discover I had seriously underestimated the popularity of the occasion because the lot

3

was completely full. Cars we re parked every which way. I thought, "Oh, My Lord! Where in the world am I going to park?" "There's gotta be *one* space left," I said, as I drove a round the lot. But there was nothing. Other guests had parked in back of the facility and along the road for about a quarter mile. But it was dark and cold. No way was I going to park that far and have to walk back ... *alone* ... in the dark ... in my drop-dead black evening dress and three-inch high heels. I said, "Oh, Lord, please help me."

It was getting later and later. I thought about just leaving, but something inside me said, "Not yet. Go around one more time." So I winded through the lot for what would be the last time: zigging and zagging up and down each row. Still nothing!

Just as I was about to give up, lo and behold, what do I see but an empty parking space --- right in front of the main entrance, no less! And, on the diagonal! "YES! YES! YES!" I shouted as I rolled into it.

(It just doesn't get much better than that, does it?)

As I waltzed up the stairs to the grand ballroom, I felt so special, even favo red. It was as if by divine appointment the party ... like the parking space ... was awaiting my arrival. I thought, "Huh, there must be something to this, because this happens to me all the time."

Here's another example:

My daughter was graduating from George Washington University, which is located in the heart of Washington, D.C.

I had the task of picking up her cap and gown, which were being distributed at the college bookstore. She was in Europe at the time and wouldn't be arriving until the day before the ceremony. The problem was the only time I could pick the items up was between 8:00 a.m. and 10:00 a.m., one of the worst times of all to be traveling into the District, not to mention finding a place to park.

As I drove up 23rd Street in bumper-to-bumper traffic and around endless construction sites, I looked for a parking space, but there wasn't one anywhere in sight. I cut across I Street and down 21st. Nothing! By now it's about 9:35 a.m. --- the tail-end of rush hour. "It seems like someone would be moving out of a spot by now," I'm thinking. But not so. I spotted one, but the light caught me and a car crossing the intersection horizontally beat me to it. The light finally changed and when I turned the corner onto H Street, there it was . . . a parking space! Wide open! Right in front of the bookstore just waiting for me. It had my name on it! And was even on my side of the street so I didn't have to do the parallel park thing!

Ahh, but it gets sweeter:

So I parked and began walking toward the meter. From the distance I could see that the red expiration flag was down, meaning there must have still been time left on it. Sure was --- 70 minutes! "Well, All right!" As my good friend Mark Cummings would say, "I was feeling pretty good about life."

I was in and out of the bookstore within forty minutes, tops. As I walked back toward my car, a driver on a similar search gestured me asking if I was leaving. When I gave him a smile and an affirming nod, I could see his mouth form the words, "All right!" I pulled out and he drove in, but I paused a couple of cars down to fasten my seat belt. Through my rearview mirror I saw him step up on the curb to feed the meter. His face expressed obvious delight when he realized there were about 30 minutes left on it. I also think it would be safe to assume that the "hi-five" he gave to his friend and the thumbs up to me meant he was feeling pretty good about it, too.

What an exhilarating little "gift" that was, wouldn't you say? Now, do you think that made his day? Who knows? It sure made mine. That's all that mattered. Even though getting to D.C. on most days can be a hassle, that brief encounter shared with a total stranger turned an ordinary day into the kind of day that leaves you with a good feeling every time you think of it.

I'm telling you, this happens to me all the time! And here is one of my all-time favorites:

Like many world-class cities around the globe, Washington, D.C., with all it's history, culture, and excitement throughout the year features a number of events that are free to the public; of course, attracting hundreds of people as only the word *free* can. One such event (actually, it's a series of concerts) presented by the United States Air Force Band at DAR Constitution Hall is The Guest Artist Series, which showcases big names like Melba Moore, Wynonna Judd, José Feliciano, Toni Tennille, Kirk Whalum, George Duke, Kool & the Gang, and Japanese jazz keyboard sensation Keiko Matsui. We're talking exceptional entertainment, here, folks ... and *free!*

Only by chance did I hear that the series was featuring Chaka Khan, one of my favorites, in the lineup of extraordinary talent. At the last minute I decided there was no way I was going to miss it. So I rendezvoused with my friends Chris and Irene at Irene's house, since she lived closest to the city, and we all drove over in one car. For ease of parking, the plan was to leave Irene's at 1:00 p.m., but because we were having so much fun, we didn't head out until about 1:20 p.m. We thought we were OK, though.

WRONG!

The concert began at 3:00 p.m. and the doors opened at 2:00. By 1:45 p.m., when we arrived, the lines were practically wrapped double around the building. They had been forming since noon. To have had even a ghost of a chance at the better seats in the house, we should have arrived far earlier than we did. To make matters worse, it appeared a parking space was not to be found any closer than a dozen city blocks in either direction.

Chris suggested that she get out to hold a place in line while Irene and I hunt for a parking space within a reasonable distance. (*Oh, and did I mention this was right after a snowstorm that had left about a foot of snow on the ground?*) We drove around and around and around, but there was nothing. People had even begun parking in illegal areas, taking the chance the police wouldn't ticket that day. That, however, was a risk I was just not willing to take. (I still have flashbacks from the horror of having my car towed and that was years ago.) We were both about ready to call it quits, pick Chris up, and just go home, but in my heart, I still believed we'd get a break. Somebody would have to move sooner or later. All I had to do was be positioned for it.

As we started around for what would be the last time, I came upon a curious-looking driveway I had to have passed a few times by now, but I don't recall seeing it before. Posted was one of those ambiguous signs (for which D.C. is infamous) seemingly indicating the lot was only for visitors of the Washington Monument. However, as I read more closely, I realized the sign didn't say that at all. It said "Parking — Washington Monument" not "Washington Monument Parking ONLY." So I drove in behind about seven other cars. Both our eyes, Irene's and mine, searched for a parking space.

Before fully entering the lot, out of the corner of my eye I saw a white parking lot line well-camouflaged by the snow around it. A car was parked to the left of the line and the area to the immediate right was completely covered over. Beyond the covered area tiny bits of grass showed through. I realized the covered area was concrete --- a parking space! The first in the row and a legitimate place to park!

We pulled into the space and hustled out of the car, overjoyed by our unlikely conquest. Everybody ahead of us missed it. Not only was it a great parking space, how about only three-blocks away from where we were going! And, we were still able to get great seats.

Yes! What a deal!

And, Chaka was B-A-D, too!

Though simplistic as they are, these three scenarios mark the point of my first epiphany that inspired the title and the writing of this book. Peculiar "happenings" like them would occur so frequently that I began to seriously take note of what appeared to be a very definite parallel. The parallel is this:

WHENEVER A NEED ARISES IN MY LIFE, GOD SENDS A CORRESPONDING PROVISION TO MEET THAT NEED—EVEN IF THE NEED IS ONLY FOR A PLACE TO PARK MY CAR!

Now, on the surface, this may not seem particularly insightful, I admit. And, in the grand scheme of things, it may even seem somewhat trite. After all, finding a parking space wasn't anything I had attached much significance to before. But, continuously finding them under the strangest set of circumstances awakened me to a profound epiphany:

THE LORD ALWAYS PROVIDES WHAT I NEED. HE ALWAYS HAS. HE ALWAYS WILL.

While contemplating that profundity, I searched the scriptures for the verse that reads:

". . . MY GOD SHALL SUPPLY ALL YOUR NEEDS ACCORDING TO HIS RICHES IN GLORY BY CHRIST JESUS." *PHILIPPIANS 4:19*

I'd read that at least a thousand times before. I know it by heart. But, this time it was as if I'd read it for the very first time. In absolute amazement, for the next few moments, all I could do was repeat over and over:

All of my needs!

Not some of my needs!

A-L-L of my needs!

"ALL" meant ALL!

All meant even a parking space!

WOW! Think about that for a moment.

I was completely blown away.

Oh sure, I've always known God was good and all. That wasn't anything new. He's come through too many times for me not to know that. The parking space scenarios just made me so much more conscious of how intimately He is involved in even the minutia of my life. They made me want to examine that intimacy more closely. And, for the first time, I began to appreciate the depths to which His care extends and *how good* and *how present* He is in my life all the time.

It suddenly became crystal clear to me just how practical God is and how comprehensively He takes care of all my needs whatever they may be (of course, not necessarily in the same way all the time). Some needs He'll take care of right away. Others, over time. But, His promise is unequivocal: "... *God shall supply all your needs according to His riches in glory by Christ Jesus.*"

That's His promise.

Talk about a paradigm shift!

This was major!

My "light bulb" (as Oprah calls it) blinked when I realized that my need for a place to park my car is just as important to Him as my needs in "more significant" circumstances. The fact that He provides for the greater (food, shelter, health, and so on), doesn't in any way diminish His regard for the lesser (i.e., a parking space). It literally changed my life and the way I looked at everything.

GOD IS ABOUT MEETING NEEDS!

The more I contemplated this, the more God began to resemble a manager of a secured parking lot with spaces to fit every size and type of vehicle imaginable. And, when we drive onto His lot (when we make Him Lord of our life by completely surrendering to His loving care), Our Heavenly Father will direct us straight to the spaces He's reserved especially for us.

Read on. I guarantee you'll never look at a parking space the same way again!

A coincidence is when God wants to remain anonymous.

Garth Brooks

TRUST AND FAITH
CHPTR2
♥ STATE OF JOY ♥

What in the World Is a Great Parking Space?

Of course, this book isn't literally about locating a great place to park your car, although it could be. At a critical time, the need for a place to park is as valid a need as any other. Spotting one can be exhilarating, especially when the prospects are bleak and you're pressed for time. Think about the last time you found a great parking space in an impossible situation. I 'll bet you that was a happy moment. Wasn't it?

So, what in the world is a great parking space, you ask?

The aforementioned scenarios and those throughout this book are metaphors for which I've nicknamed "Great Parking Spaces," or "GPS" (pronounced "Jeeps").

Now until recently, most people associated the term GPS only with the sophisticated computer technol-

13

ogy used to track the movement of people and objects around the world, underwater, and in outer space. But, the GPSs I'm talking about stand for God's inexhaustible grace expressed through the undeserved miracles, blessings, breaks, and bonuses He showers on us every day to encourage our hearts and meet our needs ... even for a place to park the car! A "great parking space" is anything — great or small — that is an answer to your prayer, puts a positive spin on your cirumstances, brings joy to your heart, or gives you peace.

A GPS is a tender hug from my daughter, the twinkle in my son's eyes, and the gentle touch of my mother's hand. It is the sound of my good friend Gracie's hearty belly-laugh whenever she greets me, or the courtesy of the stranger who allowed me to merge into traffic this morning seconds before the Woodrow Wilson Bridge span opened. It's that cozy feeling I get sipping a cup of coffee (with French vanilla flavoring) by the ocean at sunrise, and the awesome pageantry of a majestic sun setting in the evening sky.

A GPS is a good night's sleep under a toasty Downey-smelling blanket; the sound of raindrops tapping on the window. It's a cool breeze brushing across my face, in summer, and the heart-melting little voice of my niece Symone, barely two years old, calling to say, "Hi, Auntie Marnet!" (That's baby talk for "Auntie Margaret"!) Regardless of how trivial they may seem or the many forms they may take, GPSs always serve the best and highest good for us in that moment.

EVERY GOOD THING IS A GPS!

Every act of kindness, every expression of love, compassion, or concern; every expression of generosity shown toward me by anyone, at any time. If it is a good thing in any shape, fashion, or form, I call it a "great parking space."

Why do I call them "Great Parking Spaces"?

I call them that because in some ways, experiences like the scenarios described resemble the elation I get when I've "lucked up" on the perfect place to park my car, especially when there was little hope in getting one at all.

Case in point:

Of all mornings, I was caught up in the worst traffic tie-up imaginable and running late for a very important meeting with the managers in my district. By the time I reached the building, the sign in front of the parking garage read "Lot Full." The next closest garage was on the other side of this mammoth complex and I had only about sixteen minutes to get parked and inside on time. By the time I found a space over there and walked back, I would have been late. So I drove past the "Lot Full" sign ... just as a car in the first row was pulling out and I got the space. I was ecstatic!

"Now, how do I get in the building?" I asked myself.

I had never been to this particular location before and wasn't sure on which floor the meeting would be taking place. There was an elevator and a door leading inside.

Both we re a few feet away from where I parked; but which one would take me in the direction I needed to go? I hadn't a clue! After a moment's contemplation, I decided to try the door --- which opened right into the corridor where my meeting was to be held! Not only did I arrive eight minutes early, I was the first one there!

That's a GPS!

Remember the time you we re sitting at that red light and the corner parking space across the intersection on your side opened up just as the light changed, and you just rolled into it?

That was a GPS!

And who can't relate to this:

It's almost 2:00 p.m. on Super Bowl Sunday, and you're in your favorite supermarket to pick up two or three things you want to enjoy while watching the game. You figure it should take only five or ten minutes to get in, out, and home befo re the game comes on, but the store is especially crowded. All the local churches have let out and it seems like eve ryone in town had the same idea as you. Only about two-thirds of the registers are open, all with lines almost stretching to the back of the store. Time is running out, and the person in front of you has a cart piled to the ceiling with at least three months wo rth of groceries. You've got about six minutes to get home in time for kick-off (and you are kicking yourself for not setting the VCR).

You are certain it will be almost half-time before you get out when suddenly you hear, "Bing!" A clerk's voice says, "I can take someone over here," and the clerk is pointing at you. "Yes!" you say as you shuffle over to her line and out the door, arriving home in time to catch the tail-end of the national anthem and kickoff.

(Or how about when the person with the loaded grocery cart turns to you and says, "Would you like to go ahead of me?")

These are all GPSs!

How'd they make you feel?

Pretty good, huh?

I'll bet you clinched your fist and went, "Yes," didn't you? Well, I sure did!

As I said, GPSs show up in our lives everyday in a variety of ways. Though you certainly didn't call them GPSs before now (but, you will from now on!), you've experienced them many, many times. A GPS can be the simple satisfaction of making all the green lights on a long busy street, finding a dollar bill on the sidewalk, or the delight of a lip-smacking meal.

You've probably never attached a whole lot of importance to experiences like these before now, have you? I know I didn't. Finding a great place to park had never been the object of any of my prayers or petitions nor were they ever included in any expression of gratitude that I can recall. As I thought about it, anytime I took inventory of my blessings, I didn't even think of these kinds of things. Quite honestly, before my epiphany, I don't recall ever thinking of something like finding a great parking space as anything other than a "lucky break"— a fluke. Yet, in retrospect, I knew something delightfully strange had happened because I felt just a little bit special.

Like this:

On a recent trip from Aruba, my flight landed in Miami within minutes of my departing connection. I ran as fast as I could to catch it, only to discover I was running in the opposite direction. By the time I made it to the correct terminal, the door to the plane was closed and the flight attendant informed me that boarding was complete and the crew was in the final stage of preparation before take-off. I walked away dejectedly, realizing I had to sleep in those hard, uncomfortable chairs in the terminal until morning because the next flight to D.C. was in six hours. Suddenly, in the quiet of the terminal, I heard, "You got your boarding pass?" I turned in the direction of the voice. It was the same flight attendant who denied me access before. "Yes," I said. "All right then," he said," Come on."

YES!

GPSs are those Aquarius moments when it seems all the stars in the universe are lined up perfectly behind you. You're in the right place at the right time — a minute sooner or later, and you would've missed it. Everything you touch turns to gold. A GPS is that "lift" you get when you've just had your hair done. And it's the snazzy way you look in that razor-sharp suit. You know the one! It's a surprise visit from a friend who owes you money. (The funny thing is that you had forgotten all about it.) It is a joke that cracks you up every time you think of it, the fresh smell of flowers watered by the morning dew, and that free feeling you get cruising down the highway on a picture-perfect day in your clean pretty car, with the top down or the sunroof open.

GPSs are sometimes wonderfully spontaneous, frilly happenings that seem to come out of nowhere but are meant just for you (or at least they seem to be). Sometimes they make you laugh out loud, or they leave you with a spacey smile that have people wondering what you're up to. Other times, they humble you to tears, leaving your heart overflowing with gratitude because the outcome of a desperate situation was what you had been praying for.

Most GPSs are so commonplace you hardly even notice them. Others so extraordinary you won't forget them as long as you live. They're the ones that define a moment and provide content for the testimony you will share with family and others for years to come.

While GPSs always serve a need of some kind, they often occur in unusual ways, and in the process elevate your appreciation for the moment and give you hope for the future.

AMAZING GRACE

Call them whatever you like . . . miracles . . . ironies . . . coincidence . . . Karma . . . a GPS is "whatever" caused you to bite your tongue just seconds before realizing your boss (of whom you were about to make an unflattering remark) was standing right behind you within earshot. And, after tearing the house apart, a GPS was that "something" that lead you to those misplaced car keys or that irreplaceable keepsake a loved one gave you just moments before they went to be with the Lord. And, when you were going under for what you thought would be the last time, a GPS was the grip of the mysterious hand you felt snatching you back to safety. You'll see the term GPS in this book most frequently used interchangeably with "blessings" because that's exactly what they are!

A GPS is simply evidence of God's amazing grace and sustaining involvement in our daily lives. Varied in size, depth, and complexity, they are the handprints of His goodness, the footprints of His mercy. And, whether they make you laugh, cry, or dance for joy, all of them are manifestations of His divine provision for whatever we need at that moment. I believe the Lord serendipitously sprinkles them in our lives everyday just to make us feel special, favored, and loved.

Though we may recognize them also as a hunch, impulse, or intuition, GPSs happen all the time, playing scarcely beneath the surface of human consciousness. Even ominous feelings of warning or danger are GPSs, and we all experience them.

I'll bet something like this has happened to you:

One morning, Ruth was about twenty minutes from home on her way to a meeting when she realized she had left her Daytimer on her desk. Thinking she could safely get through the morning without it, she resolved to keep her appointment and go home afterward to get it. As she continued to drive, an increasing uneasiness about her calendar compelled her to take the next exit and go back to get it. As she put her key in the door, she was hit with the distinct odor of something burning. Following the smell, Ruth ran up the stairs as fast as she could to find the iron lying face-down on the floor, still on, just beginning to singe the carpet.

I shutter to think what would've happened had those feelings not overtaken Ruth urging her to return home when she did. My mother calls these kinds of GPSs "whispers from God," and some are. But, this was a shout!

I heard a "voice" once warn me to catch the car door seconds before it slammed shut almost locking the keys inside with the motor running. A "feeling" once moved me to look outside where my daughter (then a child) was playing just in time to catch her getting ready to step off the curb into the street. These kinds of GPSs urge us to take a specific action, even though at the time we may not understand why. But, our understanding isn't necessary — action is, so God has to yell sometime to get our attention, as in Ruth's case. Only when we get to glory will we discover how often we were rescued by His mysterious hand.

When you went to bed worried out of your mind and

"something" woke you up in the middle of the night with the answer to the problem you'd been wrestling with, that was a GPS. When "the doors" mysteriously opened and the tide of distress took an unexplainable turn in the other direction, that was a GPS, too. GPSs were the times the Lord made a way out of no way; the times He rescued you from disaster so sure, you knew it couldn't have been anyone else . . . and it certainly wasn't you! As when . . .

Several years ago, the doctor ordered a mammogram for a friend of mine named Kathy as part of a routine physical. The X-rays returned with a noticeable shadow on one breast, indicating what appeared to be a sizeable tumor—the last thing any woman wants to hear. Consistent with protocol, a more comprehensive mammogram was ordered the next day. Feeling certain it was nothing, the doctor still scheduled a biopsy for the following week. Having been a graduate registered nurse for more than thirty years ("millions" as she puts it), Kathy knew what that meant. She'd seen others go through the same thing many times before.

From the time Kathy left the doctor's office, she could hardly eat or sleep or think of anything else. If the diagnosis was positive, some tough decisions would have to be made.

Early one morning, after a particularly restless night, Kathy got a phone call from the doctor with the most extraordinary news. The second mammogram did not show any sign of a tumor. While reviewing both sets of her X-rays, it was discovered that the first set had been misread. As it turned out, the shadow on the film was found to have come from a warm coffee mug that had been mistakenly placed on the envelope the film was in.

Kathy didn't have a tumor after all!

Visibly overcome with tremendous relief, she could barely bellow a tearful, "Thank you, Jesus!"

TENDER MERCIES

Most of us can easily picture God showing up for something such as feeding the hungry, healing the sick, and making sure the earth continues to revolve on its axis around the sun. We can relate to Him showing up, for instance, with help on September 11. You wouldn't be surprised if He shows up at an earthquake or other natural disaster. That's all very important stuff. You might say that the Lord might even think it's important to show up when the engine in the car blows up, you lose your job, or your spouse walks out on you, this time for good. After all, He's God and that's what God does—takes care of big stuff!

But, we don't imagine an awesome, mighty God showing up just as faithfully when a parking space or a break in the line at the supermarket is needed. We just don't! Who would ever think of God as a parking valet or a supermarket cashier? No one! (Unless, of course, you've had my epiphany!) Yet, that's exactly how He shows up when that's what's needed. That's because God is everything you need!

Is it love you need? Then God is love (1 John 4:8, 16)! You need peace? He's the Prince of Peace (Isaiah 9:6)!

Need a friend? He'll stick closer than a brother (Proverbs 18:24). A parking space? I think you get it. God is whatever you need, and here's a great example of just that fact:

Every writer who has ever attempted a literary undertaking of any kind is occasionally paralyzed by what is commonly referred to as "writer's block" — you sit there staring at a blank page and can't think of a single thing to write. That's exactly where I was in this work when out of nowhere came a GPS I will remember and cherish forever.

I wanted a story to convey just how much God is in tune with our needs in every situation, and I simply couldn't think of anything that didn't sound corny. I was sitting at my desk, looking out the full-glass door, when up walks my son, Darnley, and his best friend, George. Darnley had recently purchased a condo in the area and had just moved back to Alexandria after having lived in Richmond while completing his degree at Virginia Commonwealth University.

They stayed for a few minutes, talking and laughing with me, and as they were leaving, I escorted them outside to the porch. Darnley gave me a big hug, as he always does, and as we walked toward his car, he put an envelope in my hand. On it was written "Mom." Curious, I began opening it, all the while saying, "What's this?" I could see it was a card with a picture of a giraffe inset in the center of the cover. As I opened it, I saw a handwritten note, and suddenly, all these $20 bills . . . $200 worth . . . began falling onto the ground. He's slowly driving off, and I'm waving this wad of money in the air with both hands, yelling, "What's this? What's this?" As I walked slowly back inside, I began reading the note, and this is what it said:

"When it comes to being thoughtful, you're heads above the rest.
THANKS!"

I have always been such a cry-baby about these kinds of things so, of course, by now I'm practically blinded by my tears. And as if that wasn't enough of a tear-jerker, read what his handwritten note said:

Hey, Nerd (our pet name for each other at home),

Thanks for helping me get into my place. I couldn't have done it without all of your help.

I just want you to know that I appreciate you and that I take nothing for granted.   I love you. Thank you from the bottom of my heart,

Darnley!

Before Darnley came that day, I had been asking the Lord for a compelling GPS story to tell. This is that story! The GPS I needed walked right in the front door in the form of my son!

The added beauty of GPSs is in the way the Lord uses them. They enable us to: (1) recognize who He is; (2) they demonstrate how inadequate we are and how sufficient He is; (3) they teach us to trust Him implicitly; and, (4) they encourage us to walk in faith and love.

All in all, GPSs are symbolic of the amazing ways Our Loving Heavenly Father lets us catch Him peeking in on our lives to assure us He's with us every moment and in every situation. They demonstrate His incredible attention to even the micro-details and illustrate the depths to which His Majesty condescends to provide what we need including the ones we often regard as too trivial to be worth bothering Him about. And, who but God could ever know how much care He takes for the needs we don't even know we have?

Now that you know what GPSs are, I'll bet you can recall quite a few of these interesting little intrigues yourself, can't you? Every day of your life, you'll experience many more GPSs, except from now on you'll appreciate them for what they really are: His wonderful tender mercies gently sprinkled over us, and His reassuring winks telling us, "It's OK. See . . . I'm right here!" Pay attention, my friend, and you'll catch Him in the act!

As you read through this book, which I hopen-will encourage your heart with the turn of every page, take comfort in my paraphrase of Matthew 6:30:

IF OUR HEAVENLY FATHER TAKES SUCH PENETRATING INTEREST IN LITTLE THINGS LIKE PARKING SPACES, HOW MUCH MORE WILL HE TAKE CARE OF THAT WHICH CONCERNS US MOST? OH, YE OF LITTLE FAITH.

**People see God everyday;
they just don't recognize
Him.**

Pearl Bailey

TRUST AND FAITH
CHPTR3
♥ STATE OF JOY ♥

Luck Has Nothing to Do With It

It was actually about two years ago that I really began to take notice of these peculiar occurrences I seem to continually experience, particularly whenever parking my car is involved. My next point of epiphany evolved when I observed a similar parallel as before (my need for a place to park), except it involved my needs in more significant circumstances. The epiphany was this.

CIRCUMSTANCES ARE ALL THE SAME!

They're all the same, because

TO GOD, THERE IS NO DIFFERENCE!

Whether it's money I need, guidance in making a tough decision, healing from an illness . . . or a place to park my car, to God, one dilemma is no more of a challenge to Him than any other.

IT'S ONLY A MATTER OF SCALE!

29

We're the ones who create this hierarchy of difficulty, in effect judging Almighty God by our meager limitations.

NOTHING IS TOO HARD FOR GOD!

And, nothing is too small or insignificant for us to forego asking Him to provide. That's why you can go to Him about *any-thing.* All human challenges require His divine hand because *"apart from [Him], we can do nothing"* (John 15:5).

WITHOUT HIM, WE CAN'T EVEN
FIND A PARKING SPACE!

As surely as He cares enough to provide a parking space (admittedly, most times, a lot less significant than quite a number of other things I can think of), He is also just as able — and willing — to provide for our greater needs when they arise. Thus, the extent of our involvement in the outcome of any situation, no matter what it is, can be narrowed down to six responses:

(1) Acknowledge our complete dependence on Him;
(2) Recognize that He is in control and is sufficient in every situations;
(3) Have faith in His character and sovereignty;
(4) Submit to His Will;
(5) Trust in His promises; and, most importantly,
(6) Obey His Word.

I used to feel "lucky" about my good fortune in finding the great parking spaces, even arrogant enough to think that I somehow had something to do with it but, never realizing God was orchestrating everything all along. And, when I say everything, I mean everything! It never occurred to me that God would be operating on what seemed such a petty level. The more the GPS scenarios played out, the more I began to expect them. It became a game for me! I knew I would get a great parking space no matter what ... and I did! Why, I was so cocky with it, I would sometimes challenge my skeptics . . . and win! When it came to finding a great place to park, I was so consistent, they even started believing it.

People who knew of my good fortune would express their confidence in me finding a space (and I'm sure used it as an inducement so I would drive). What's more, if the parking space I found had a meter, it usually had time left on it! Now my family and friends use the term *great parking space*, or GPS, on a daily basis to mean every positive experience they encounter in life. Almost everyday my kids or someone will call to share a terrific GPS story, like this one from Erica:

About an hour and a half before she was to leave for a seminar she was to give to a group of employees at the CIA, Erica decided to make a few changes in the display of transparencies she would be using—a simple adjustment of the computer file. She clicked on "print" and waited for the twelve pages to begin to come through, then left the room to continue final preparations. Once she heard the printer stop, she went into her office expecting to retrieve her beautiful documents, but instead discovered an absolute horror. The transparencies she used were for a laser printer not an ink-jet like hers, making the transparencies unusable. In a panic, she looked in her office supply cabinet to see if she had any transparencies left from the last time she printed them successfully and thankfully, found eleven. "Great!" But, she needed twelve! With that, she decided to delete the least necessary transparency (the last one) and clicked to print again.

Thinking she was set to go, she left the room again. But when she returned to retrieve her transparencies, she discovered that the first page—her title page—did not print because her printer was set to print the first page last. By this time, it was getting really late, and she had to leave. There was no time to run down to the business supply store and buy more, but she knew her presentation would look awkward with the title page missing. After a few moments she thought to check the supply cabinet again and began looking into everything that would possibly hold transparencies. She came upon an unmarked manila folder that was way in the back. Inside were six transparencies.

Erica was able to print her title page and arrived in plenty of time to deliver a successful presentation.

PRAISE THE LORD!

Do you think for one minute that God didn't know about Erica's impending dilemma? Well, He knew, all right! He not only knows all, but He is all, and he had already prepared a GPS for Erica left in the form of an unmarked manila folder hidden in back of a cabinet, not to be opened until the day coinciding with her need for them.

GOD . . . SURPRISED? HARDLY.

Luck, you say? I don't think so! The Lord is on top of everything! Why? Because, God is the source of it all and He *always* provides for everyone who puts their trust in Him. I don't know about you, but this gives me considerable peace.

So, you see,

LUCK HAS NOTHING TO DO WITH IT!

Let everything be a blessing;
It will put your heart to rest.
Let everything be a blessing,
And you will always be bless'd.

Joy Hart

TRUST AND FAITH
CHPTR4
♥ STATE OF JOY ♥

The Three Kinds of GPSs

As you can see by now, GPSs manifest themselves in a variety of ways. Yet, for all their varied manifestations each one is distinguished by its own unique characteristics and falls into one of three categories: the "Yes GPS," the "Hallelujah GPS," and the "Whew GPS."

THE "YES GPS"

"Yes GPSs" are the serendipitous happenings that seem to come from out of nowhere but, of course, don't. They're among the easiest GPSs to recognize because they are always joyfully uplifting. A resounding "Yes!" "All right!" "Yippee!", or "Right on!" usually follows a Yes GPS experience. Anyone within a few feet of you will know you've had one. The Yes GPSs leaves you with somewhat of an assurance that "someone is looking out for you", that "someone's got your back." Yes GPSs often function as little pressure valves designed to relieve immediate stress like that derived from catching a train just seconds before it

35

leaves the platform.

The Yes GPS is the "break" life gives sometimes to encourage us and remind us that there is hope and that life really is a very good thing.

Take this for example:

In the spring of 1993, my friend Sandy, a divo rced mother of a pre-schooler and a second grader, was down to her last dollar during a particularly tough time when there was more month than money remaining. She was running out of even the essentials (milk, toilet paper, Pampers) and trying desperately to hold on until pay d ay, which was three days aw ay. She figured if she didn't go anywhere unnecessarily, she'd at least have enough gas to get back and forth to work and still have a few dollars left to buy lunch for the older child.

On this particular morning, Sandy was at her wit's end. The weather was unseasonably cold, so she grabbed a jacket out of the hall closet and headed out to make her w ay through the normal snarled rush-hour traffic, all the while praying for relief. She needed something to happen --- a miracle, I suppose, because she was at her breaking point and didn't know what she was going to do.

When she arr i ved at the garage where she parks every day, she got out and locked it as she usually did. When she placed her keys in her pocket, she felt her hand rest on something that felt like paper. As she withdrew her hand, her fingers we re wrapped around, of all things, an

ATM receipt ... and three crisp $20 bills! "Praise the Lord! $60!" she cried as she danced unashamedly beside her car for a moment or two shouting "Yes! Yes! Yes!" "Thank you, Jesus!" People were looking at her strangely, probably thinking she had either lost her mind or hit the lottery or something; and, in a strange way, she had. However, the most remarkable thing is this: the receipt was dated February 13, 1990.

Sandy hadn't worn that coat in almost three years!

What a terrific Yes GPSs! A classic. Isn't that just like God?

In his infinite wisdom, the Lord knew what Sandy would need that day. Oh sure, she needed money all right. But, on that day, she needed encouragement as much as anything. She needed to hear from Him in a real and tangible way. And, true to form, in response to her need, He showed up at just the right moment and with just the right dose of encouragement, administered in a powerful and memorable way. Sandy told me that even now, just thinking about that day brings tears to her eyes ... *and that was more than ten years ago!*

Yes GPSs like these are the filling stations that dispense just enough spiritual and emotional fuel to get you to the next station of hope and opportunity. They are a boost to the spirit and they empower you with the faith to go on when you feel like giving up. A Yes GPS can change your whole life . . . at least for that day! Sometimes, that's all you need.

THE "HALLELUJAH GPS"

Hallelujah is the highest exaltation of praise one can give to God. In fact, it is the mantra inexhaustibly sang by the angels in Heaven to glorify His holy and wondrous name.

So, what exactly is a Hallelujah GPS?

"Hallelujah GPSs" are the unmistakable events that only God alone can engineer; the opportunities and circumstances only He can create or change. Their supernatural dimension is painfully obvious even to non-believers. Their origin points straight to Heaven — the only source of the truly miraculous. Whoever said, "He may not come when you want Him but, He's always right on time," knew well what a Hallelujah GPS was. Hallelujah GPSs distinguishably magnify the Lord's sovereignty in situations that are impossible to us. In fact,

THE GREATER THE IMPOSSIBILITY, THE GREATER HIS MAGNIFICENCE.

Hallelujah GPSs are the unquestionable miracles: the undeniable super-blessings that leave you gasping almost in disbelief. They are like "dreams with your eyes open" because the miracle is being played out right in front of you. They're hard to fathom because the nature of a Hallelujah GPS is indeed unfathomable in and of itself far exceeding anything we could ask for or imagine. If you're not a believer when one happens to you, a Hallelujah GPS will make you one, or at least have you thinking real seriously about it. Many times they are the solid answers to prayers that have been desperately and persistently prayed.

So, you still don't believe in miracles? Well, let me tell you about Cherry Valley then.

Back in the late 80's, early '90's, I left the company I was working for to start my own business. Things were moving along very well. My client-base was growing and the future looked bright. Then came Operation Desert Storm, the war in the Middle East, causing everyone to put the brakes on spending for almost any reason, and my little business took a tumble like you wouldn't believe. The need to find an alternative source of income like *NOW* was fiercely upon me. My daughter was at Boston University (not a piece of chump change, believe me!) and my son was in middle school and involved in a number of extracurricular activities that were very expensive.

It took a while, but I finally found a job in commission sales again (where I had previously found tremendous success) that over time became quite lucrative. At the moment, however, it was still a serious struggle to meet some hefty obligations. By the time I got to where I could see my way clear again, my house was in foreclosure and creditors were hounding me relentlessly from morning until night. My excellent credit rating (something I had always been very proud of) took me from hero to zero and the little money I had saved was finished. I was in desperate trouble. The slick greasy walls of my rut made it impossible to escape on my own. I was drowning. And I was scared to death. I went to work --- hard --- all the while trying to maintain a normal "on top of it" persona in my job as well as at home for the sake of my children. Where my job was concerned, it wasn't their business. As for my children, well, kids draw their sense of security from their parents' behavior, so I never wanted them to feel threatened by knowing we were literally about to have our stuff set out on the sidewalk. They were innocent. It wasn't their problem to solve. It was mine, and I was determined to protect them at all costs.

I would go to bed sick with worry. My pillow would be soaked with tears as I buried my face in it to muffle the sound of my terrified cry before the Lord so the kids couldn't hear me. During the day, I would drive out to the gardens on the outer perimeters of the property where I worked and plead for the Lord's intervention, then compose myself and return looking like I had it going on.

I kept getting notices from my mortgage company threatening me with their intent to foreclose, so I knew I had only a few months to turn things around. During that time, I saved as much money as I could for a down payment on a rental property and moving expenses. Expecting rent would cost about $1,200–$1,300 per month, I estimated the minimum amount I would need to move would be about $5,000. I asked God not to let us be evicted, at least not before I had $5,000 saved.

As it got closer and closer to the eviction date, I started looking for a place. I told the Lord I wanted it to be a single-family house with four bedrooms, at least two full bathrooms, a two-car garage, and within walking distance to Mount Vernon High School, where my son would be attending. (He once said he wanted to graduate from the school his sister graduated from.) Every place I considered, the owner understandably wanted to do a credit check—something I dreaded, because I knew my history and was afraid they would reject me on the spot. Though nice, none of the houses I had seen were the ideal anyway. I hadn't quite saved enough money to move yet, so I just kept working, saving, and looking.

Then one Saturday morning in May, I was in my office. It was a very quiet morning, so I began perusing the classifieds. I noticed this house listed for rent in one of the most sought-after neighborhoods in the area, literally right across the street from the high school. I called the number to get the street address so I could drive past it first to see if it would be something I would be happy with.

Well, indeed it was!

I slowly drove past the house three or four times, affirming and reaffirming my satisfaction. The front door was open and I could see someone was standing inside watching me as I drove by. The person finally came to the door, so I decided I would stop and politely ask him about the property. The person turned out to be the owner, and he was there waiting for someone who had made an appointment to see the house, and he thought I was the appointment. I explained to him I was not the person with the appointment, but I did have an interest in the house. He invited me to go ahead and look around since the other person wasn't there, so I did.

Talk about being nearly perfect: the house was only one bedroom and one garage short of my ideal, and only three blocks from my son's school. Careful not to appear impolite and stay too long, I thanked him for letting me tour his house and told him I would follow up early the next week.

The following Tuesday morning, I called him and was informed that the other people never showed up. I told him I liked the house and would be interested in a rental arrangement. He told me he would fax the application over to me and I could return it to him by Wednesday. Dread immediately set in because I knew the credit issue would surface and we were running dangerously close to the eviction date. Fortunately, the previous week had been extremely lucrative and, with what I had saved, I had more than the $5,000 I thought I would need to move.

When I retrieved the fax from the machine I gasped in amazement. It was the most unusual application I had ever seen in my life. Besides asking for my name, the names and ages of my children, my place and length of employment, and the license number of my car, he asked nothing else! He didn't even ask for my current address, home phone number or my social security number. He made a phone call to my employer to verify that I indeed worked there and called me back before the day was over offering me a rental arrangement. The word "credit" never even came up!

Have you ever heard of such a thing?

Two days later, on Friday at 3:15 in the afternoon, I met the owner at the house to sign the lease and give him the security deposit and two months' rent (he only required one). When I went home that day to the house we were losing, taped to my front door was the Sheriff's final notice of eviction that would take place in five days. The noted time of service was 3:15 p.m. ... the same time I signed the lease for our new house!

The foreclosure did in fact proceed on my property, but by the time it did, we were safely and securely in our beautiful new house on Cherry Valley Lane. The six years spent there were some of the happiest and most memorable years of our lives. I was never late paying, the owner never once raised the rent, and Darnley got to graduate from the high school his sister had graduated from. The Lord indeed gave us everything we needed and much, much more than we could ever have asked for.

HALLELUJAH! PRAISE THE LORD FROM WHOM ALL GPSS FLOW!

Cherry Valley was the most incredible, supernatural blessing I've ever witnessed because I saw the Lord respond in answer to a specific and desperate plea. Before we moved in, I called three friends who were aware of what I had been going through and said to them, "You have got to come over and see for yourself what the Lord has done for Margaret!" They came. To this day, whenever I speak with them, they will still recall the amazing way the Lord moved in my situation and how blessed they were to have seen it first hand.

Though they occur less frequently than a Yes GPS or a Whew GPS (the next topic), Hallelujah GPSs are so extraordinary that you have to tell somebody! In fact, you'd probably be hard-pressed to keep it to yourself even if you wanted to. The testimonies they generate are so powerful one should be hard pressed to refrain from telling anyone who would listen. Why, I've been so excited over a GPS, I've told perfect strangers like when:

In December 1999, my daughter Beverly graduated from George Washington University in D.C. with a Masters degree. Rather than immediately accepting an elevated position in her field (international event production), she decided to enroll in a nine-month language immersion program abroad to not only refine her proficiency in the three languages she speaks already (Spanish, French, and Italian), but also to become imore familiar with the culture --- fabulous credentials for her profession.

Determined to do this, she searched relentlessly for a way to make it happen and discovered a program on the West Coast through which she could enroll with a post-graduate degree and still qualify for the financial assistance she needed to pull this off. She submitted all the information they needed to determine her eligibility, and within a short time they awarded her a financial package that would cover all her expenses abroad as well as her expenses here in the States. Beverly owns her home, has a lease on a new car, and all the expenses that go with both. Never once did I doubt this would work out for her. Beverly is a very determined individual and when she sets out to accomplish something, the intensity of her focus is like a bulldog's grasp on a piece of raw meat. She becomes visibly transfixed. You can see the determination in her eyes and in her behavior: she walks faster, her eyes gleam. She is "focus" personified. But, beyond what I wanted, and beyond her intense pursuit, I knew the Lord wanted this for her, too. Why would he not want something this wonderful for her? This was such a good thing!

Bev was all set to leave on January 22, 2000, and the few weeks prior to her departure were filled with lots of shopping and packing. She submitted her notice of resignation as Director of Marketing for the event production company she was working for and tying up loose ends. I had told the world about this because something this wonderful had to be shared. Everyone was so excited for her and the well-wishes were pouring in. My daughter was on her way to Europe, where she would live for three months in Spain, three months in Italy, and three in Paris. Except for relatives who had been in the military, no one in my family had ever experienced world travel like this. We were all vicariously set to live this adventure with her.

About four days before her departure, during the final frenzy of making sure she had everything she needed and was ready to go, I was upstairs when I suddenly heard the most pitiful crying. I ran to see what the matter was and found Bev sobbing pitifully over a letter that had come in the mail. It was from the financial aid office rescinding her award. She was devastated. It didn't make any sense to me. Our expectations for this happening were so high; so sure. I couldn't have dreamed anything else was possible. This was not happening!

I *knew* the Lord wanted her to go. She had worked so hard and had been so creative and efficient in her planning. She found discount student fares for air and rail travel that would take her all over Europe, Greece, Turkey, Africa, and the Mediterranean, to name a few. She had lined up hostels and hotels in the various cities. And we had prayed about this. There was no way this was not going to happen for her. No way! I couldn't believe it would go like that. She was ready to leave!

I left her there for a moment in her despair and went upstairs. After a minute or so, I came back with my Bible and I said to her, "Come here, Sweetheart. It's time to get out the big guns." We sat down together there on the stairs and I reminded her that God was in control; that this upset was nothing more than an illusion, a lie from Satan designed to discourage her and undermine her faith. I told her that the Lord knew the situation and I believed He had already worked things out. I knew He had because we both had gone into this venture in prayer and God is faithful. I told her there was no way the Lord would have brought her that far just to leave her.

GOD IS NOT A PRACTICAL JOKER!

Though indeed a demonic scenario, it was also a fantastic opportunity for her to see God demonstrate His awesome power on her behalf before her very own eyes. I proceeded to read these passages of scripture to her:

"And all things, whatsoever ye shall ask in prayer, believing, ye shall receive."

Matthew 21:22

"And we know that all things work together for good to them that love God, to them who are the called according to His purpose."

Romans 8:28

"Now unto Him who is able to do exceeding abundantly above all that we can ask or think, according to the power that worketh in us."

Ephesians 3:20

And,

"And this is the confidence that we have in Him: that, if we ask anything according to His will, He heareth us (v. 15) and if we know that He hear us, whatsoever we ask, we know that we have the petitions that we desired of Him."

1 John 5:14-15

Then we held hands and prayed together. In a spirit of praise, we began thanking him for making the way clear for her to go abroad as planned. We told the Lord how much we believed it was His will for her to go and that we had acted on that belief with justified expectation. In complete confidence, I told her to get up and continue packing without giving any thought to anything except praise and thanks to the Lord for working it out.

Two days before she was to leave, we got the word we had been expecting. An official from the school called to inform her that the letter had been sent in error and that her financing had been approved. Funds in the amount of more than $25,000 had already been wired to her account!

Praise the Lord! Hallelujah!

On Saturday, January 22, 2000, my baby was on Air France en route to Barcelona, Spain!

This was undeniably nothing short of a miracle! You must know that no one could have possibly done that but the Lord God Almighty.

OH, WHAT A MIGHTY GOD WE SERVE!

Three months later, Beverly was traveling to Milan, Italy, to rendezvous with friends and wasn't having any success finding a reasonably priced hotel. Everything had been booked because there was a holiday of some sort going on that she was not aware of. As she shared with me the difficulty she was experiencing, I assured her that she was bound to find something because [she interrupted me saying], "I know, Mom . . ."

"I ALWAYS GET A GREAT PARKING SPACE!"

The next day she emailed to tell me that not only did she find a great hotel in the heart of Milan but, that the cost was even less than the lowest fare offered by the student travel office!

GPSs, especially the Hallelujah kind, are meant to be as much of a blessing to others as they are to the one experiencing it. That's why you must tell somebody.

"LET THE REDEEMED OF THE LORD SAY SO!" PSALM 107:2

Sharing your own personal story of how God has brought you through is unmistakably the most powerful medium available through which anyone can illustrate how real He is and for teaching others to recognize the many ways He shows up in the daily lives of those who trust Him. Like the angels who sing, "Glory to God in the Highest," GPSs continually affirm,

HE IS WORTHY TO BE PRAISED!

Anytime you experience a phenomenal GPS you must tell others about it. They need to know.

THE "WHEW GPS"

A "Whew GPS" is the miraculous avoidance of what might have otherwise been a dangerous or unfortunate situation. These are the close calls, the dodged bullets, and the near-misses that can upstage your entire life within a single moment evoking the long-winded alleviating "Whew!" sound we make when we've narrowly escaped disaster.

Unlike the exuberant Yes GPSs which are almost always immediately, enthusiastically, and generously shared with others, the reaction to Whew GPSs is usually more solemn and often delayed. There's a good chance you might not share them with anyone except the Lord ... *ever*, or at least not for a while. Whew GPSs can send you immediately into shock or into deep contemplation and reveal penetrating issues about life in general (or your life in particular). Whew GPSs will force you stop and think!

When I was about seventeen years old, I was driving my mother's car through the Hampton Roads Tunnel that runs between Hampton and Norfolk, Virginia. In those days the tunnel had only two lanes --- one in each direction --- and the speed limit was 75 mph. Having received my driver's license on the first try the year before, I imagined myself an "experienced" driver.

It was a warm summer day and a great day for driving. I was by myself, confidently cruising, laid back with one hand on the steering wheel and my head bobbing as I sang along with the tunes on the radio.

For whatever reason, probably to change the station or to get something out of my purse, I took my eyes off the road for only a moment. The instant my eyes returned to the road, in a blur I saw this object dash from in front of my car into the lane of traffic moving in the opposite direction. That blurred object was a car on the wrong side of the road (my side) passing the car in front of it. There couldn't have been ten feet between us.

"WHEWWWW!!!!"

Numb and in a state of shock, I had no choice but to continue driving because there was no shoulder area inside the tunnel on which to stop safely. When I reached the Norfolk side, I pulled into the parking lot of a restaurant at the water's edge. As I sat there looking out over the water, I cried for at least an hour. My faith wasn't as strong then as it is now, but I knew that the Lord had spared me. Were it not for His Grace alone, the cars would have collided head-on at a speed greater than 75 mph, undoubtedly instantly killing everyone involved. I wouldn't have known what hit me, and I certainly wouldn't have been around to tell this story.

Oddly enough, I don't recalling telling this story publicly before now. But, I'll never forget it and it's been more than thirty years.

PRAISE GOD FROM WHOM ALL GPSs FLOW!

Similarly, on my twenty-seventh birthday, I was driving along on the Connecticut Turnpike and had entered the city limits of New Haven, just beyond the West Haven toll gate (the toll gates have since been torn down). "Herby," our 1976 silver Volkswagen Bug and I were cruising steadily at about 65 mph in the express lane next to an eighteen-wheeler that was in the middle of this three-lane stretch of highway. The truck was about a hundred feet ahead of me when suddenly its cab abruptly lunged forward and jackknifed squarely in front of me. Herby was a five-speed and I was breaking those gears down for all I was worth and managed to stop within about three feet of the cab (which by now was in my lane facing me) without crashing into it head-on.

"WHEWWWW!"

Thank God the driver behind me was able to stop in time to avoid rear ending me and sandwiching me between the car and the tractor trailer.

Whew GPSs usually teach valuable lessons. The lesson here:

God is in complete control!

He alone gives life and He alone takes it . . . even if it is your birthday! Only by His Grace do we "live, breath, and have our being" (Acts 17:28) certainly not by anything we do that's for sure.

By now, you should be able to see why even backing out of your driveway and making it safely from one end of the street to the other each day is an event to be celebrated. We usually don't specifically pray to not be killed in a head-on collision with an eighteen-wheeler, at least not until you've had a close call like mine. But remember,

GPSs are often answers to prayers we don't ask or even know to ask. We take so much for granted. Yet, God in his inexhaustible mercy continues to bless us for reasons known only to him.

Whew GPSs also manifest in less dramatic ways, as when you are spared from embarrassment or regrettable behavior: for instance, when you are sooooo sure *you're* right and *they're* wrong. This is always damning. Let me illustrate:

Periodically, I transfer an amount equivalent to necessary expenses from my money market account at one financial institution to my checking account at my credit union. I accomplish these transactions usually by mail or on-line because the credit union is a considerable distance away from my home, and I try not to go there in person unless it's absolutely necessary. On this occasion, as usual, I mailed in a check for $2,400 marked "for deposit only" and left town for the Labor Day weekend. Mail is almost always received and posted by the next business day.

While away, I called the Auto-teller to confirm my balance, which showed an amount considerably less than $2,400. Because I could retrieve my transaction information over the phone, I requested a listing of the most recent transactions and the computer relayed the following: "Your share draft transaction list is on August 31: electronic funds withdrawal of $43.44; draft 0000 of $36.65 was paid on August 31; September 1, deposit of $24.00 was posted; on September 2, ATM withdrawal of $60," etc., etc. It did not list the $2,400 deposit. I thought, "I'll just check again when I get home". It probably didn't arrive in the credit union's mail until after closeout and will likely show up the next business day, which is Tuesday (Monday was Labor Day).

I returned home three days later on Tuesday and called the Auto-teller again. Still no $2,400 deposit. My next call was to a live human being who confirmed the same information as the Auto-teller. Their records showed a deposit on September 1 of $24 and the transaction was handled by one of their most experienced people. I explained that I mailed a check for $2,400, as I usually did, so there must be a mistake [of course, on their part]. I never made a deposit for as little as $24 on September 1, nor on any other day for that matter. Then it hit me! THEY must have misread my check and credited the wrong amount. That's what the $24 was all about.

Just as I was about to get up on my high-horse and assume that posture of righteous indignation for *their* apparent incompetence which could have been responsible for setting off a domino effect of bounced checks, including the mortgage, that voice inside me said, "Margaret, keep cool and get all the facts before rushing to judgment." So, I stayed cool. Still righteous, but cool.

Restrained by that voice, in an outward pretense of courtesy, I asked the representative if he would send me a copy of the $24 check, which would certainly establish the fact that *they* had made a humongous mistake.

Though I wanted to prove them wrong, I wanted to do it in a dignified, smirky manner. After all, I was a longstanding valued customer.

Two days later, the check copy arrived in the mail. The amount written on the check was "Twenty-four ——— 00/100" . . . in my own handwriting!

WHEWWWW!!!

(And I thought I had gotten a handle on my arrogance and my propensity to want to be right. It seems I've still got a lot of work to do in that area so . . . back to the drawing board!)

> *"Thank you, Lord, for your Grace that saved me*
> *from making an absolute fool of myself and*
> *offending one of your precious children."*

Some wake up and say,
"Good morning, Lord!"
Others wake up and say,
"Good Lord, its morning!"

Anonymous

TRUST AND FAITH
CHPTR5
♥ STATE OF JOY ♥

Your OutLook Equals Your OutCome (YOL= YOC)

If we would only slow down a bit, we'd experience more GPSs and see them happening to us and around us all the time—even now, at this very moment!

Oh, you don't see them?

Well, consider this: your heart is beating, isn't it?

You're breathing on your own, aren't you?

Chances are you can walk and talk, right?

You're able to read this, right?

And, most obvious, **YOU WOKE UP THIS MORNING!** (If not, then you're dead, and it doesn't matter anyway!)

Regardless of your circumstances or the state of your health right now, if the activities named above are the only events occurring in your life, I would say you should consider yourself among the highly blessed because . . .

It could've been the other way!

Things could be much worse ... *a lot worse*. We are blessed with so many privileges; privileges we so easily take for granted. They are showered upon us every day, and they're what make life so worthwhile.

Oh yeah, it can get pretty rough out there. Still, each new day greets us with its own wonderful cache of GPSs, all of which can encourage us as we experience life's unique variety of unpredictable scenarios. Despite everything, the sun is still shining. The sky is still blue. The stars will in all likelihood twinkle tonight by the light of the silvery moon. There's probably food in your refrigerator, and, although on its last leg, "Old Betsy" hasn't quit on you yet. Nor did the bad news you were expecting ever come.

At the end of each day, most of us would have to admit we have a lot to be thankful for and good reason to feel hopeful about the future.

Just do the math!

Admittedly, seeing a GPS is easier on some days than it is on others. So, just as you would search the lot for a great parking space (perfect location, easy entry, easy exit, etc.), there are going to be days when you have to search hard for GPSs, too. They're there, all right! You just have to dig a little deeper to find them. And, in doing so, you must have an outlook of positive expectation because your outcome will most surely be the equivalent.

Surprised? I can't imagine why.

How you see the world and view life events is a function of the decisions you make about how you're going to think. That, I'm afraid, is the reality . . . we really do create our own!

Far surpassing all other factors that construct your reality, your attitude will determine your outlook, which in turn will influence the outcomes you experience. When you choose an outlook of positive expectation (optimism) over an outlook of negative expectation (pessimism), the positive outcomes you desire become more viable and more likely. Thus, PTs + PEs = POCs:

POSITIVE THOUGHTS + POSITIVE EXPECTATIONS = POSITIVE OUTCOMES

Conversely, negative thoughts usually precede negative expectations, which usually precede a negative outcome. Thus, NTs + NEs = NOCs:

NEGATIVE THOUGHTS + NEGATIVE EXPECTATIONS = NEGATIVE OUTCOMES

In both cases, we create a self-fulfilling prophecy. Ultimately, it is *you* who decides if events and circumstances are a blessing or a curse. If you choose to view life from the standpoint of positive expectation (and you really do choose), you'll begin to see blessings in even the smallest events and in the worst of circumstances. Negative expectations distort the view.

The next scenario demonstrates this well.

Years ago, I worked for a major cemetery company as a counselor and periodically worked on Sundays in rotation with two others. Although sometimes busy, Sundays were usually very quiet and the office was open only until noon. A couple of people would came in to make a payment on their account, but most would inquire about the location of the resting place of a loved one. I would usually bring a good book to kick back with while I enjoyed the peaceful, quiet solitude.

On one particular Sunday morning, it was raining heavily and not one soul came in (at least not one I could see!). My office had huge windows that spanned the height of the room from floor to ceiling and my desk was positioned so that I could easily see outside. The day was dark and a thick fog cast a gray quietness over the miles of beautiful green rolling hills that lie before me, creating a cozy, cuddly kind of ambiance. A crackling fire in the fireplace would have completed the setting very nicely. (I'm sure you're beginning to think I'm a little weird, but a well-maintained cemetery is one of the most peaceful and beautiful settings in the world. Visit one sometime and see.)

As I settled in to take full advantage of this opportunity to spend some wonderful undisturbed quiet time, the phone rang. It was the general manager. "Boy," he said, "What a rotten day this is. If you're not busy, just lock up and go home and get out of this mess. This is an awful, awful day!"

His reaction was so categorically opposite mine that it startled me. Without thinking, I said, "A bad day? What in the world is a bad day? How can there be such a thing! Any day that I can drive through those gates not riding behind someone I love, and, as important, every day no one is riding behind me, I say that's a good day! How could there ever be any such thing as a bad day whenever you get one?"

He said, "Huh, I hadn't thought of it that way. You've got the right attitude, Margaret. Go ahead, stay as long as you like." That's exactly what I did, and I enjoyed a wonderful day.

Humans are the only creatures to which God gave the ability to affect the quality of the day — even destiny — by the exercise of our free will in the choices we make about what we expect. And this universal truth constantly applies:

You [GENERALLY] GET WHAT YOU EXPECT.

Since thoughts have the power to project any outcome you desire, you can expect anything you want — even if you don't get it! Doesn't it then make sense to project the outcome most desired? So, why not?

Go for the positive!

What in the world do you have to lose? You've got at least a 50-50 shot at it being either way, especially in circumstances you can't control. There's nothing wrong with expecting a desirable outcome, if it's a good thing. There's actually a lot about it that's right. It's the only healthy alternative.

In Washington, DC, it is not uncommon to have to park a distance away from an event unless you arrive early. I never feel that the prospects of finding a great parking space are hopeless. But, I also know pessimists who will immediately begin to whine and complain should they fail to see one right away. They anticipate having to walk too far in the cold, or in the heat, or the drizzle, or in whatever conditions their negative imagination generates. Seldom do pessimists entertain the possibility that they'll get where they want to go at just the right time — that a great parking space is waiting for them or that everything is going to work out fine. Many times they're even surprised by a favorable outcome. (More about negative people in Chapter 6.)

I'm an unapologetic, hopelessly perpetual optimist. Folks know me for my optimism, and they can usually count on me for a "shot in the arm" or a reassuring admonition when they find themselves headed down the slippery slopes. I simply believe things are always going to work out for the better. Nevertheless, I've known people — pessimistic people — to express irritation at me because of what they refer to as my "sickening optimism."

Imagine that!

Why I've even had people ask me with a tone of irritation, "Don't you ever have a bad day?" My answer is, "No."

(I've already told you why.)

This is not to say that I always know how things are going to work out. Most times I don't have a clue. But, I have faith. I know the Lord hears my prayers. For believers, troubles are often worked out long before any physical manifestation is evident. For example, when Daniel prayed and fasted for knowledge on behalf of his people, the moment his words reached God's ear, a heavenly being was *immediately* dispatched in response (Daniel 10:12).

The Bible, in both the Old and the New Testaments, is replete with example after example of God's faithfulness. They were put there to reinforce our faith and to foster the positive outcomes we should expect if we claim we are Children of the King. This is not to say that God will always answer us the very moment we call, but He promised He would take care of us and that He'd never leave us alone (Hebrews 13:5). He is faithful to deliver us from negative circumstances when we put our trust in Him for as long as it takes.

Ninety percent of what most people worry about never happens. Seldom are things truly as bad as they seem once the initial shock wears off and the dust settles. It's a matter of perspective—a matter of attitude having to do with the way we *think* about what's happening around us.

As a child, I grew up in a very large family: my mother, my father, one brother, five sisters, and Aunt Geneva, my father's elderly cousin. From my earliest remembrance around the age of five, I wanted to graduate from high school and get a college degree. As a matter of fact, I didn't want just one degree, I wanted two: a bachelor's and a master's. And I wanted them both by the time I turned twenty-seven years old.

Only my sister Kathy and my cousin Curtis Albert had gone beyond high school. Still, I never had even the slightest doubt that I would go. My father had only an eighth-grade education, but he was a brilliant, self-taught man. My mother, now in her mid eighties, finished high school—a major accomplishment for an African-American daughter of a sharecropper seventy years ago. Why it wasn't until I began the application process that I even understood that to go to college one had to have money—even to apply! Well, my parents didn't have any money and, Lord knows, I surely didn't. The issue of money just never occurred to me. I didn't know from where, but I knew the money would come.

Fortunately, I had a brain. I was smart and eager. Being a smart poor kid became my saving grace. Through the guidance office at my high school, I discovered I was eligible for tuition assistance through scholarships and grants. I was even eligible for application fee waivers! For all the years of study at the undergraduate level, I owed only $400 of the thousands of it took to educate me to that point. I graduated cum laude with a bachelor's degree and four years later, received an M.B.A. ... three months before my twenty-seventh birthday ... just as I expected to.

To me, the glass is always half full, and I truly believe with all my heart that "all things work together for [my] good . . ." (Romans 8:28). That's what the Bible says. That's what I have to believe to keep moving on. I *expect* to find something good in and about every day. And, I do! I *expect* to be where I'm supposed to be when I'm supposed to be there. And, I am! I *expect* my interactions with people I encounter to be positive. And, they are! I *expect* to travel up and down the highway without incident. I *expect* to have my needs met. And, they are! And I *expect* to get a great parking space — and I do every time! Positive expectations correspond directly with the frequent practice of observing God's faithfulness and His ever-constant attention to the details of our lives so much so even "the very hairs on [my] head are numbered" (Luke 12:7).

Once I was able to understand the relationship between my thought process, my attitude, and my outcomes, a remarkable peace settled over me. It changed everything! I'm seldom in the fanatical hurry I used to be in trying "to make things happen." I don't take negative things so personally anymore and I am a lot less likely to get upset when I find a situation is not to my liking. Rather, I've grown more confident in the truth of His love and in the fact that I can expect His absolute best. In every circumstance now, I start looking for Him, trying to see what He's up to in my life. I don't frighten quite as easily as I used to when I don't readily see a solution to a problem. This is because I know the Lord is in full control.

HE IS THE SOLUTION!

Instead of staring at the problem like a deer caught in the headlights of an on-coming car, I've learned during those times to "seek [Him] first [knowing] all these things will be added [unto me]" (Matthew 6:33).

My life changed for good when I *made the decision* to start believing Him and all the wonderful promises in His Word. With that attitude, what other outcome could there be for me but a positive one? What could it be for you? Ultimately, I'm where I'm supposed to be, when I'm supposed to be there. A great parking space is *always* reserved for me. And, so is yours.

So start expecting good things. Make the decision to expect a positive outcome in the challenges you face today. Expect happiness, success, kindness, generosity, peace, and love. And ...

"Whatever things are true, whatever things are honest, just, lovely, of good rapport; if there be any virtue or praise, think on these things.
(Philippians 4:8)

Expect good things to happen for you and they will! What will make it happen is your prevailing positive thoughts and your faith in the character and faithfulness of the God who made you and who cannot lie (Titus 1:2); the God who was totally sincere when He said, "I will *never* leave you nor forsake you" (Joshua 1:5). Once you "*get it*," you'll have little trouble recognizing a GPS in any situation. From here on out, if you don't see all the wonderful GPSs happening in your life every day, even when the thunderclouds are forming, examine first the way you're choosing to look at the world because:

YOL= YOC EVERY TIME!

GOT IT?

GOT IT!

**A wonderful life is the sum
total of every blessing
received over a lifetime,
regardless of how long or
short that life might be.**

Margaret-Ann Bogerty

TRUST AND FAITH
CHPTR6
♥ STATE OF JOY ♥

Eleven Reasons We Miss the Great Parking Spaces

Let me reiterate. GPSs are *blessings*—of all kinds—often cloaked in varied and sundry disguises. But, because we often expect blessings to only show up in certain ways, its the ones of a material nature that get our attention the most like hearing our name called as the winner of the latest Power Ball drawing.

Of course, it would be a tremendous blessing if our proverbial ship reaches shore with such fortune. However, the reality for most of us is that those humongous GPSs occur much too infrequently, if at all, to allow our peace, happiness, and joy to hinge on them. Too often when the blessings don't show up quite big enough or when, how, and where we want them to, we become disappointed suffering all sorts of self-imposed unhappiness. But, we should never feel short-changed because our GPSs don't always show up as dollar bills. Instead, we should be open to gratefully receive a blessing any way and any time it comes.

I've never heard of anyone in their final moments asking for their laptop, investment portfolio, or the keys to the Mercedes 600. (of course, there's a lot I haven't heard of!)? For most people, what usually counts most in the tally of a meaningful life is family and friends who truly love them, good health, a clear conscience, divine protection, and a good reputation. And, when it's time for you and me to cross Jordan, it will be the multiple little GPSs sustaining the precious memories we share with those who care.

Let's take a look at the eleven top reasons we often miss the great parking spaces.

REASON ONE

WE CAN'T SEE FOR LOOKING

When I was a little girl, my mother would sometimes send me on an errand somewhere to retrieve an item of some kind. I'd be looking for it, but sometimes I just didn't see it. In frustration, she'd finally come upstairs or wherever and walk right to it. With the item in hand, she'd say to me, "Child, you can't see for looking."

Our attention is often so clouded by distractions of all kinds that we sometimes can't see obvious blessings causing us to miss GPSs all the time. Sometimes we see them but, like a penny on the sidewalk, we step right over them not recognizing them for the treasures they are. Some of the most priceless GPSs show up in very ordinary ways and can add joy and enrichment to your life — something we all need all the time. The thing to remember is that enough little GPSs can produce a lifetime of happiness that can more than compensate for all the big ships that never quite make it to shore.

It is imperative for us to recognize GPSs at every occasion and passionately embrace them when we do. When it's all said and done, it will be the countless number of little GPSs compiled over a lifetime that will make up the preponderance of what you and I hold dear. True happiness lies in the memories GPSs create, the laughter they generate, and the peace they bring to your heart whether your ship ever comes in or not. In fact, when you stop to consider how blessed you are on all fronts regardless of your circumstances, you should quickly realize that your ship comes in every day you fog up the mirror. If that doesn't change your outlook for the better . . . *you've got a lot of work to do!*

REASON TWO

WHAT YOU SEE IS WHAT YOU GET

A *premise* is a cognitive intellectual mechanism humans use to evaluate life situations in order to form opinions about themselves, other people, their environment, circumstances, even God. They are our underlying beliefs and assumptions forming the backdrop for our interpretations and reactions to life and our ability to recognize or *really* appreciate anything.

Remember "YOL = YOC"?

Well, in much the same way, a positive premise will naturally create a positive interpretation of circumstances whatever they are. A negative premise will correspondingly conform. Because we each decide *how* we interpret what happens to us and around us, the formulation of a premise, whether positive or negative, is an *elective* undertaking we exercise according to our own choosing. Once a premise is identified, it is *our* decision about whether or not we will continue to accept it or change it. A change in your premise will automatically change your interpretations and reactions, ultimately your outcomes.

What premises are you laboring under?

One of my sustaining life premises, which I actually mentioned before, is this:

EVERY DAY IS A "GOOD" DAY IF YOU GET ONE!

I hear people all the time talking about the *bad day* they had or expect to have. This confuses me greatly. The term *bad day* in my mind is on its face an oxymoron when viewed through properly adjusted lenses. How could any day you wake up alive and breathing be anything but fantastic? It doesn't get any better than that! If that event doesn't occur, do you realize what that would mean? Have you ever really considered the impact the failure of that critical event alone would have on your calendar?

Seriously! Too many people complain that today it's raining or it's not raining. It's too cold or too hot. As for me, I'll take a day any way I can get one because the alternative is the ultimate disruption.

Naturally, it would be great to go through each day with everything moving along the way we'd like. Life, unfortunately, just isn't like that. We have to take the sun and the rain. Just because everything may not be going right doesn't mean *everything* is wrong either. It's still a good day! You have to define what a good day is every day to at least a minimum criterion. Being alive is my minimum! Having a pulse! For me, if I only get to wake up and feel the bright warm sun shining in my face in the morning, I say that's a *mighty* fine day! And, if that is absolutely the only blessing I get; if not another good thing happens to me all day long (as if that were possible) then Praise the Lord! "This is the day the Lord has made. I will rejoice and be glad in it!"(Psalm 118: 24). I'll take it anyway it comes because:

THE WAY YOU SEE LIFE IS THE WAY YOU'LL GET IT.

Without a minimum criterion of life satisfaction we can easily lose sight of God's goodness and mercy. Each day is like no other day before it nor will it be like any day after it. The experiences that occurred yesterday or today probably won't occur tomorrow, at least not exactly. So, before trashing the day as a waste or categorizing it as "bad" (a description that actually reflects more about your attitude than that of any genuine connection to reality), take a moment and survey all the beauty the Lord has placed around you: the loved ones He's given to cherish you, and the provisions He's made for you however meager they may be. Look for blessings everywhere and in everything because they are everywhere and in everything. Even through chaos or crisis, concentrate on all that is going right in your life and "in everything give thanks, for this is the will of God in Christ Jesus concerning you" (I Thessolonians 5:18).

And, if there be but one thought you take from this book, let it be this one:

THERE IS NO SUCH THING AS A "BAD" DAY ... ANYTIME YOU GET ONE!

Any day His grace wakes you up with a reasonable portion of health and strength, and warm blood is running through your veins; any day His wings of protection shadow your children and loved ones; any day He has kept evil from you and is with you at every turn, that's a SUPER DAY!!! Anything beyond that is a bonus.

JUST BEING ALIVE IS THE GREATEST PARKING SPACE I KNOW!

REASON THREE

"THE SPIN CYCLE"

Have you ever noticed how the washing machine snatches your clothes from the top of the barrel and drags them down beneath the water? Then, the next cycle kicks in draining the water out? Finally, the last cycle sends them into a swirling spin to get rid of the water that's left? Well, that's exactly what negative people will do to you if you're not careful. They'll snatch you and drag you down into their frenzy of issues, drain every drop of your positive energy, and before you know it, you're spinning in a cycle of someone else's confusion, frustration, aggravation, and failure without even understanding how you got there. I call it *The Spin Cycle* and it's a trap you need to recognize and avoid at all cost.

Next to your own negative outlook, the negative reactions of other people pose the greatest threat to the wonderful possibilities of would-be-nice life experiences. How much more enjoyable and fulfilling would life be were it not for negative people? Sometimes they are your boss, your spouse, your parents, even the cashier at the store. Unfortunately,

NEGATIVE PEOPLE ARE EVERYWHERE.

They are your "trusted friends" who waste your time by calling to tell you what they heard about Sally Sue's mother's third husband's niece in Arkansas (information, of course, received from a "very reliable source"). They are the hypocondriacs whose exaggerated condition worsens with each retelling of their sad story. They criticize everyone and complain about everything. And being proponents of the "truth" (which, coming from them, will always be negative), they're the first ones to tell you ("*in love*," of course) how impossible your dreams are and how surely you're going to fail. After all, "no one has done it before and somebody needs to give you a reality check." But, whose reality?

Look at this:

My friend Mark and I once owned a used-car business. We called it "Ride 4 Under 5" because our inventory included only well-running vehicles that cost $5,000 or less. We parked our cars on a lot along the main highway with pertinent vehicle information and a "For Sale" sign with our telephone number prominently displayed in the window.

One afternoon I received a call from a woman expressing an interest in one of the vehicles and who wanted to see it more closely. "Great!" I said. "Why don't I meet you at the lot and you can look it over and take a test drive, if you like." She was fine with that, but explained she didn't have a car but was on a bus route and could meet me in about an hour. I asked her where she lived and she proceeded to tell me her address, which turned out to be less than a mile from me. On that note, perceiving her to be a sincere buyer, I offered to pick her up and she accepted.

When I knocked on the door, a child about seven years old answered and announced my arrival. As I entered the house, I could see there were more children, all between the ages of five and seventeen. I introduced myself to the woman and we chatted a bit as she got herself together to leave. When asked if all the kids were hers she proudly answered, "Yes—all five!" She was barely thirty years old, unmarried, and pregnant with number six.

The seventeen-year-old, a daughter, came with us. They looked the car over, took it for a test drive, and upon returning stated she wanted to buy it. While processing the paperwork, I engaged the daughter in light conversation such as one would have with a seventeen-year-old: what school do you attend, when will you graduate, what are your plans for college, what do you think you want to study, etc. You could easily see the excitement in her face as she expressed her ambition to study journalism and become a foreign news correspondent.

Being the academician that I am, I was thrilled and began to encourage her with talk of the opportunities for extensive travel she'll have, the excitement of meeting different and important people, and being there when major news events happened, and so on. I said to the woman, "You must be very proud of your daughter," who was obviously an ambitious, intelligent, and well-spoken young lady. However, I was amazed at her response and, to be honest, pretty darned disgusted.

Sadly shaking her head from side to side, the mother said, "I can't see it. I just can't see it!" I went on about why it was such a good thing as if I had a personal stake in it (in a way, I did). I pointed out all the wonderful possibilities her daughter's choice could have for her and move her beyond her present circumstances. Mom wasn't persuaded. She simply repeated again, still shaking her head, "I can't see it. I just can't see it. I'm sorry but, I just can't see it!"

About two years later, I ran into the mother in the supermarket and inquired about her daughter, who at that moment came from out of another aisle --- pregnant with her second child.

I guess she couldn't see it either. Her dreams obviously abandoned for her mother's "*reality*."

Driving is something from which I derive considerable pleasure. Because I do enjoy the experience so much, I'm somewhat guarded about whom I permit to participate in that experience, particularly if it involves some distance. Occasionly, I may have a colleague or a friend or two riding with me to lunch or to a seminar or somewhere. Even more rarely, I may ride with them. But, I generally prefer to ride alone. That way I'm pretty much guaranteed a positive driving experience barring any unforeseen upset on the road.

Now, if it is my kids riding with me or maybe a few others, the probability of a fabulous trip increases substantially regardless of who is driving. With them a usual trip is an adventure and big fun because they are positive people with flexible dispositions.

I frequently use the highway as somewhat of an unscientific empirical laboratory. It is one of my favorite places to observe behavior and over the years I've noticed some pretty interesting things drivers do that to some extent reflect their personalities and state of mind. A ride of only a few miles will usually give me ample opportunity to observe their behavior and draw certain conclusions about their self-concept and their outlook. Both really show through behind the wheel of a car. My conclusions from these little experiments have not only helped me become a better driver, they help preserve my enjoyment of the driving experience. Here's what I've concluded from my unscientific highway laboratory.

People with a generally positive life outlook will usually have a corresponding positive self-concept demonstrated in a few ways; that is, they have a healthy opinion of themselves. They are usually courteous to other drivers allowing them to change lanes smoothly. They share the road. They don't dominate or intimidate other drivers, or try to. To their passengers, they are considerate inquiring as to their comfort and will make reasonable adjustments to accommodate them just as they would in their home. They are the ones cruising along at a safe steady pace probably listening to their favorite music while taking in the view, or laughing and talking with whoever is riding with them. They move with the flow, but aren't particularly rushed and appear to be confident about where they're going.

Conversely, people with a generally negative life outlook and corresponding self-concept are more easily identifiable. They're the ones trying to squeeze you out as you attempt to merge into traffic. When you turn your signal on, they're the ones who speed up to keep you from getting in front of them causing you to miss or almost miss your exit. You'll see them barreling down the highway at a break-neck speed, riding the bumper of the car in front of them, and recklessly changing lanes (principal factors in the growing number of accidents and violence occurring these days on highways around the country). And, yes, they're the ones leaning angrily on the horn, upset that traffic has stopped for a moment to let an old woman with a walker cross the street.

I don't want to give you the impression that only negative people show up on the highways or that their behavior is always expressed in an angry or aggressive manner. Definitely not true. But, negative people have deep problems that can cause them to miss out on many wonderful GPSs. Like the mother of the would-be journalist, negative people are everywhere.

Negative people can be so demented that when others do nice things for them their suspicious and paranoid way of thinking causes them to believe there must be a catch — that the motives behind the gesture are somehow tainted. How often have you heard them respond with, "This can't be real?" or perhaps respond to a compliment by saying something like, "Oh, you don't really mean that."

What's important for everyone to understand about negative people is that seldom does their negative disposition have anything to do with you. True, it may *affect* you (if you let it) but it's usually not really personal. Negativity is a learned behavior usually born out of a poor self-concept and practiced for so long it's become part of the personality. It's who they are and it speaks volumes about them without really saying anything about you. But, it is not the behavior of others by which we are judged anyway.

WE ARE JUDGED BY HOW WE RESPOND.

It is up to you to find a civilized way to cope and prosper despite them because they can impact your life. What you need to do is to pray for them and show them compassion but, don't make their problems your problem. Whatever is going on with them, don't let them steal your GPSs by getting you caught up in their cycle of issues.

REASON FOUR

PRIDE

There is nothing that renders a person more incapable of recognizing GPSs than pride. Though replete with man's sins and transgressions, all of which are objectionable to a Holy God, the Bible lists pride at the top of the seven sins He hates most (Proverbs 6:16-17). Why? Because pride denounces God's sovereignty and encourages an individual to depend on himself rather than on God. Only as the need dictates, and at the sole discretion of the individual, will a prideful person consider God's wisdom as anything beyond a suggestion.

Ironically, despite knowing how detestable pride is to the Lord, people often take great pride in the fact that they are "proud people." Go figure! We've all known or heard of people who, although in obvious need, but for their pride will decline the earnest assistance offered by others who are sincerely willing to help. It is pride that we let stand in the way of our asking even God sometimes for the things we need. The price we've paid for pride is another one of those things we won't know until we reach Heaven. But, one thing I can say with relative certainty,

PRIDE IS COSTLY!

It has cost relationships, opportunities, peace of mind, even our health — and GPSs!

Pride will cause people to even qualify the way the Lord chooses to bless them. Oh, they want the blessing all right, so long as it comes on their terms, that is, through certain people or in a certain way. In arrogance they will accept a gift and in the same breath curse the gift-giver suggesting that the gift falls short of expectations or that the recipient somehow deserves better. We are admonished

"TO NOT THINK OF [ONE] SELF MORE HIGHLY THAN [ONE] OUGHT TO THINK" ROMANS 12:3

Pride catapults our self-concept far beyond what it ought to be.

Not since Christ came the first time, and not until He comes again, will God step down from His Heavenly throne to attend to us personally. God's love and help comes through people — all kinds of people — a fact prideful people have a problem acknowledging.

TO REJECT THE HELP OF OTHERS IS TO REJECT GOD HIMSELF.

And, in doing so, you may very well be blocking your own GPSs. None of us knows who the Lord will use to bless us.

Take this situation:

Once, while visiting our home, a guest became horrified to the point of hysteria because I sent my son to our neighbor's for an egg. It was about nine o' clock at night. In our close-knit little neighborhood, this was commonplace. Most of us had little children. It was a lot more convenient to borrow something you needed from a neighbor than to round up all the kids and drag them to the store at some odd hour.

So, what do you do at 7:00 a.m. when you discover there's no milk for the kid's cereal and you have to be at work in 45 minutes?

You call your neighbor!

We loaned each other eggs, milk, bread ... even whole sandwiches! That was the kind of friendship we had. We helped each other. And, we were close --- like neighbors should be. I thank God for them and I'm sure they thanked Him for me.

My guest was beside themselves when I shared that. In absolute disgust, they went on to state that, "Before I would let the neighbors know I needed them for anything, I would get a wooden bill and join the chickens!" The thought of anyone knowing they were in need of anything, especially essentials, was something they simply couldn't fathom.

I suppose that's their choice, but I think it's sad. They would surely have keeled over dead the morning one of my neighbors and I rummaged through pocketbooks, dresser drawers, coat pockets, and car seats to put together enough money to buy gas to get to work one payday many years ago.

WHEN IT COMES TO P-R-I-D-E, LOOK WHO'S IN THE MIDDLE!

REASON FIVE

INGRATITUDE

This email was sent to me recently. I don't know who the author is, and I take no credit.

St. Peter met a newly arrived soul at the entrance gate of Heaven for a tour of the buildings and grounds. When they reached the end of the tour, the soul noticed how large the last building was compared to all the others he'd seen. It seemed to be a workroom filled with angels and he wanted to go inside. Despite St. Peter's vehement attempts to dissuade him, the soul was insistent, so they went inside.

They stopped at the first section and St. Peter said, "This is the Receiving Section. Here, all the petitions to God said in prayer are received." The soul was clearly impressed with how terribly busy all the angels were sorting out petitions written from people all over the world.

They continued the tour and when they reached the second section, St. Peter announced, "This is the Packing and Delivery Section. Here, the blessings people on earth asked for are packed and delivered." The soul was equally impressed with how busy that room was, which also had just as many angels working in it as the first busily packing the millions of blessings in preparation for delivery to Earth.

Continuing to the final section of the building, the soul stopped surprised that only one angel was there idly standing by doing nothing. "This is the Acknowledgment Section," St. Peter said. The soul asked St. Peter, "How is it that there is no work here?" "That's the sad thing," St. Peter responded. "Usually, after people receive the blessings they ask for, very few send back acknowledgments of gratitude." "How does one acknowledge God's blessing?" The angel replied, "One simply says thank you."

The great majority of my working life has been spent in commission sales which provided another incredible platform from which to observe people and to draw conclusions about behavior and values. Having worked with hundreds of clients, one such observance is that the clients most satisfied with the purchase experience were the ones who could recognize when they had gotten a good deal.

On the other hand, there were those who wouldn't recognize a good deal if it sat on them. They were the ones who would rather spend a beautiful weekend dragging the wife, the kids, and the dog in and out of every business around the Beltway spending hours grinding down every salesperson they meet to get a price $10 lower than the first deal they had. How counterproductive is that? In doing so, they forfeit the opportunity of just being together as a family and doing things that *really* bring joy to those they love. What they didn't understand was this:

PART OF GETTING A GOOD DEAL IS RECOGNIZING WHEN YOU'VE GOT ONE.

And, part of having a wonderful life is recognizing that life isn't a good deal. It's a great deal! Life is a big thing! Everything else pales beside it which should in and of itself fill each of us with tremendous joy. If you can't be grateful for just that, how can you possibly be grateful for anything else, especially a little old parking space?

LIFE IS A WONDERFUL THING.

BE GRATEFUL AND ENJOY IT!

REASON SIX

COMPLAINING

I'm not perfect but, complaining is something I almost never do for a few reasons. First, no one wants to hear it. Second, even if they hear it, they are most likely powerless to do anything about it. Third, in light of all the goodness of God, what in the world is there to complain about?

Complaining is the birth-child of ingratitude and an affront to the wisdom, sovereignty, and grace of God. Like ingratitude, complaining suggests a knowledge superior to God's; that what God is doing (or not doing) isn't adequate, and that there must be a better way to get things handled. Often the good that a complainer does see is severely restricted. Their response to life will always be, *"Yes, but"* while they insistently demand adjustments more readily conformed to *their* will and timing than that of God's.

Consider the children of Israel. God set them free from their cruel Egyptian captors, parted the Red Sea so they could cross on dry land, destroyed their enemies, sent food from heaven, caused water to gush from a rock, and gave them a land full of milk and honey. Having seen all these miracles, you would think they would've trusted God without question. Did it ever occur to them that manna was a diet of special nutrients created especially for them because of the severe desert conditions they faced? That the minerals and fiber it contained were essential to keeping them healthy, strong, and free of sickness and disease? *"Yes, but . . ."*

You would think they would have noticed how comfortable their clothes and shoes were and how those items never wore out in all that time. "*Yes, but . . .*" Instead, they complained bitterly infuriating God to the point of anger that threatened their very destruction save for Moses' petition on their behalf. Yet with the dawn of each morning, God's faithfulness was so great He continued to guide them: as a cloud by day and as fire by night (Exodus 32:11-14). Their constant complaining extended what would have been a fourteen-day journey into a pilgrimage of forty years in a desert where a whole generation died without ever seeing the Promised Land.

We read the Israelites' account in the Old Testament with detached amazement appalled and frustrated by their perpetual murmuring. We readily condemn them for their ingratitude and constant complaining but, in all the wilderness events God has brought you through, how often do you allow Him to hear your murmuring, echoing your distrust? And, like the Israelites, how often do you question His sovereignty and faithfulness?

God sent His innocent Son — His only son — to die a cruel, painful death on Calvary's cross for a world of sin He never committed. And, as if that weren't enough, God raised Him from the dead so we could have the hope of the eternity He has prepared for those who have put their trust in Him. And we complain? What more does He have to do to show you how much He cares?

Examine a photograph of yourself taken ten years ago. Look at how slim you were. Oh, really? You didn't say that back then. Back then you weren't satisfied with your looks one bit. Back then you whined constantly about how flabby your thighs were and how wide your rearend was because today your frame of reference is a ten-years-younger-you. Back then you didn't know how good you had it. Today you'd kill for that girlish figure! I know I would. But, ten years from now you'll still be complaining about how you will look then. Just like before, you won't realize how great you look today. Looking back, somehow those thighs and hips don't look as bad as you thought. Complaining distorts your outlook by focusing much too much on narrow details and it causes us to miss the big picture.

I used to work out at a gym and would see people come in with these "bodies to die for" and would wonder what in the world they were doing there. I saw tiny women religiously working out on the stepper or the treadmill for hours at a time to "trim the fat." My reaction was usually, "What fat?" as they struggled to pinch an eighth of an inch between their fingers to show me. ("You're kidding?" I'm thinking. "You think that's fat? I'll show you some fat"!) No matter how perfect their bodies looked, they could always point to a flaw that fueled their insatiable desire to be "perfect." They were never satisfied. I doubt if they could ever be. But, can we?

Complaining is more than just a lack of appreciation and dissatisfaction. It is lack of contentment in its purist form. It dishonors God because it says to Him! I don't believe you!" When His faithfulness should be so obvious. It is an egregious vote of "no confidence" in His promises to keep us in all our ways.

Complaining downplays God's remarkable track

record, restricts our testimony to others, distorts the truth of His love, and robs Him of the praise and glory for which He is worthy. Just as surely as it is impossible to please God without faith (Hebrews 11:6),

IT'S IMPOSSIBLE TO PRAISE GOD AND COMPLAIN AT THE SAME TIME.

How does one stop complaining, you ask?

YOU PRAISE THE LORD!

You give thanks for what He has done, is doing, and is going to do, and you praise His Holy Name!

"LET EVERYTHING THAT HAS BREATH PRAISE THE LORD!" PSALM 150:6

It's that simple.

REASON SEVEN

CRITICISM

I may not be much of a complainer but, I have to be honest with you. I'm a Virgo and anyone who knows one knows that if there were a contest for this disgusting habit, I would probably take the blue ribbon. And, a *habit* is exactly what it is.

While many people suffer from an inferiority complex, Virgos are plagued with a complex of superiority, convinced that their views about almost everything are essential to the very perpetuation of mankind. (No ego issues here, huh? Yeah, right!) Amazingly, for years I thought it was a virtue. Moreover, I thought it was *my duty* to point out the errors, omissions, and fallacies of the world. And, who better than someone as capable and as generously endowed as I?

WRONG!

Thankfully, what I finally discovered was this:

NOBODY LIKES CRITICISM!

Nobody likes it. Even if you're right . . . even *if they know* you're right . . . even if you are trying to be helpful . . . even if it is asked for. There's something about criticism that makes people recoil. It just rubs you the wrong way.

Oh, you don't believe me?

Then ask someone who cares about you (someone who you know will be completely honest with you) if that "get-up" you're wearing makes you look fat or if that hair-do makes your head look too big. (Of course, every husband on the globe knows all too well not to touch that one!) In some instances, even when invited, people who receive criticism will frequently respond with resentment. And, unsolicited criticism can be even more dangerous perhaps down-right lethal. The criticizer may run the risk of becoming a target of unsuspecting retaliation (i.e., alienation, abandonment . . . burnt dinner!), especially by you sneaky passive-aggressive types.

What is your reaction to criticism — invited and uninvited? Drop me a note at my email address

(powermrktg@aol.com) and share with me your reaction and the truth about how it makes you feel.

Criticism says more about you than it says about whoever you're criticizing. And, you can be sure there will be few GPSs evolving from the use of it. God only knows how many family members, friends and associates I have alienated (or lost altogether) before finally learning that life lesson not so long ago. I'm sure people around me are happy about that. Even when it comes from someone who you know has your best interest at heart (and may God help the ones who don't!), there is just something in the nature of human beings that make taking criticism, at the very least, uncomfortable. May I never know the number of daggers aimed at my back because of my helpful "sharing."

CRITICISM IS SELDOM APPRECIATED.

REASON EIGHT

SELFISHNESS — W.I.F.M.

"YOU CAN HOLD YOUR FIST TIGHTLY AND SURELY NOTHING WILL GET OUT; AS SURELY, NOTHING CAN GET IN EITHER."
MY FATHER, THE LATE KENNETH MILES BOGERTY

Regretfully, countless individuals miss incredible GPSs for this one reason alone — selfishness. While nearly all of the GPSs we enjoy come through the care and love expressed by others toward us, these shortsighted, self-absorbed, self-centered individuals seem incapable of understanding the true joy one receives in giving. These are the "takers" of the world. Oh, they very much enjoy being on the receiving end of things but very little, if anything, can ever be expected from them in terms of appreciation or reciprocation.

Takers look upon givers as "suckers" worthy only of their contempt and as someone to be exploited. Whatever a taker does for anyone at any time (which may even include occasional giving), you can rest assured that it is somehow to their advantage to do so. The taker is tuned into only one station: WIFM — *What's in it for me!* The world revolves around them. And, the word "self-sacrifice" is a concept of idiotic proportion.

Well, I guess you could call me a big sucker then. I know of no greater joy than the expression of sincere appreciation and gratitude on the face of another human being because of something I've done for them or given to them. There is nothing like it in the world! I wish I were in a position to give even more. Anyone can take and receiving is good, too. But, the words of our Savior declare it much "more blessed to give than to receive" (Acts 20:35).

What the self-absorbed fail to realize is that for all their greedy and selfish grabbing to get as much as they can while giving as little as possible, with a little bit of respect and human compassion, they could get so much more.

REASON NINE

STARING IN THE REARVIEW MIRROR

Sometimes feelings of guilt, shame, or unforgiveness about something in our past can cause us to feel unworthy, disabling our ability to feel deserving of any good or positive thing. Subsequently, we miss out. That's why it's vitally important to remember where all negative feelings come from. They come from Satan. And, if he can manipulate you into believing his lies, he'll have little trouble convincing you of the futility in looking optimistically towards the future.

Driving forward while staring in the rearview mirror (which is exactly what you're doing when you focus too much on the past) will eventually result in a horrific crash. No responsible person would attempt it for very long. The habit of fixating on past failures or missed opportunities and revisiting unfortunate circumstances deserves a lot of the credit for undermining positive expectations. To be sure, understanding the past is important because the past holds valuable information that can be beneficial to the future. But,

THE PAST DOES NOT EQUAL THE FUTURE!

What happened yesterday doesn't necessarily bear on what will happen today or tomorrow. Our destiny is shaped by the choices we make each day. Each day is a new opportunity to make better choices for a better outcome and a brighter future.

If you arrived home and found your house on fire, you might have time to run in and save your children and perhaps grab a few other important things: vital records, pictures, or some keepsakes. You certainly wouldn't linger. You'd rush in and out as quickly as possible because remaining inside for too long puts you in danger of being buried under the rubble when the flaming roof caves in.

Examining the past should be approached in much the same way. If you must revisit it, run in and run out! Get what you need as quickly as you can and get out! Don't hang around lamenting about the "shouda," "wouda," "coudas." Yesterday is gone. Nothing can be done about it. Look back only long enough and far enough to understand what happened, the part you played in it, and get over it! We all have something we regret, but what's done is done. To move past negative emotions and circumstances we have to focus on the future with faith. Jesus has forgiven you. It's time to forgive others and yourself. Learn from the past what you need to learn and move forward with a positive eye toward the future.

STOP LIVING IN THE PAST!

REASON TEN

GETTING AHEAD OF GOD

You know the age-old expression, "You can't see the forest for the trees?" Well, this is about not seeing the lot for the cars! Too often we miss the GPSs of today because we're focused too much on tomorrow.

Tomorrow!

Tomorrow! You may not even be here!

Tomorrow isn't promised to any of us!

Every day is a beautifully wrapped package filled with its own experiences, presents, and surprises unique to that day. We get upset with God because He won't show us what's going to happen tomorrow or next week, next year --- or ten years from now! What we must understand is that God is under no obligation to bare full disclosure of His plans to us. He's the preeminent one! For believers, this journey is a faith walk. As Stormie Omartian says in her book of the same title, [He gives] "Just Enough Light For The Step I'm On."

ANXIETY ABOUT TOMORROW MEANS YOU'RE NOT TRUSTING GOD FOR TODAY.

We are admonished in Matthew 6:31 to "Take no thought for the morrow." Lord knows, even that's more than we can handle. Learn to take it one day at a time because

> **"YESTERDAY IS HISTORY.**
> **TOMORROW, A MYSTERY.**
> **TODAY IS A GIFT.**
> **THAT'S WHY IT'S CALLED THE 'PRESENT.' "**
> *BABATUNDE OLANJI*

Live and savor every moment of this wonderful present called "Today." Life isn't a dress rehearsal, you know.

REASON ELEVEN

"THE CHICKEN LITTLE SYNDROME"

Akin to the self-indulgent habit of complaining, the "Chicken Little Syndrome" is the tendency to invent problems where there aren't any. The more common names for this malady are "pessimism" and "worry." People with this problem are able to see only the worst possible outcome because they manufacture it. To some, the concept of positive expectation is an idea as far away as the planet Jupiter. To them, the sky is always falling. And, you know that light at the end of the tunnel? It's a train! Disaster is always straight ahead. The sunny side of the street is really a grate over a fiery furnace. The slightest inconvenience or disappointment means the end of the world.

You know people like that, don't you?

Of course you do.

Their conversation alone gives them away. Every thought is expressed in negative absolutes such as "always" (accept for the title of this book!), "never," "all," and "every" as they verbally paint the entire world with broad brushstrokes of skepticism, suspicion, and paranoia.

People plagued by the Chicken Little Syndrome can rapidly highlight every conceivable way a situation is doomed. Despite facts to the contrary, or any amount of encouragement from others, they hold fast to illusions of defeat fully expecting to fall flat on their faces, quite often quitting before they even get started. Phrases such as, "It won't work," "It can't work", "What's the use? "It's never been done before," and, "What's wrong?" are a few of their favorites. When Chicken Littles don't find a great parking space right away, they immediately conclude they'll never get one ultimately abandoning the search without realizing something my father said to me years and years ago:

"When you surrender, you lose."

Whenever you give up, you've lost!

The Chicken Little Syndrome is sometimes a legitimate feeling of simply being overwhelmed by extreme circumstances. It's when everything around you seems to be falling apart layer by layer as if the sky itself were falling (no — *crashing!*) in on top of you. I've felt that way many times, especially when the circumstances were beyond my control. Again, I'm human. It's hard to see a great parking space or anything else positive under those circumstances. Yet regardless of how difficult things were, once I composed myself, took a deep breath, and said a prayer, it became easier to absorb the truth in what the great and wise philosopher Kathleen Johnson Walker (my sister) would say when I went whining to her with my sad story:

"The heavens will not fall."

And, she was right! The heavens didn't fall. The sun still shined as brightly as ever. The moon still lit up the dark black sky. The stars continued to twinkle in the night. Suddenly things didn't seem quite as hopeless as I had imagined. With that perspective, my issues seemed a little bit smaller. Right now, just repeating the phrase in my head gives me comfort in the reality of God's sovereignty and His divine control over everything including what's on my plate. It quiets my spirit and gives me peace. "The heavens will not fall" means that regardless of how big your problem may be, our God is bigger, and He still sits high and mightily on the throne. He will not let Satan get the best of us.

Whenever you begin to feel overwhelmed, rest in the fact that God is in control. Look up! The heavens are still there, aren't they? The sky isn't falling! Is it? You must have faith that God is who He says He is, and that He'll do what He said He'd do. Once you've accepted that as a fact, that's when it's time to get your praise dance on because *it's already all right!*

**Each day comes
bearing its own gifts.
Untie the ribbons.**

Ruth Ann Schabaker

TRUST AND FAITH

CHPTR7

♥ STATE OF JOY ♥

Where in the World Are the Great Parking Spaces?

Next to the question, "*What in the world is a great parking space?*" The runner-up is, "*Where in the world are they?*". These are indeed the right questions for anyone who desires a more satisfying life every day. How does one begin to see all the GPS on reserve for them; all the wonderful ways the Lord is blessing them, even now at this very moment? GPSs are everywhere and show up in a variety of forms. Some are obvious but, many (if not most) require a more open mind to appreciate. Recognizing GPS, as with any significant life endeavor, begins first with the right attitude.

SHIFT YOUR PARADIGM

By the age of ten, a person's values are locked in place. By the age of twenty, all values are acquired. Earlier I wrote about the importance of adopting a positive premise—a positive assumption—about life. Remember, "*There's no such thing as a bad day whenever you get one?*" Well, akin to adopting a positive premise is the *decision* to change the way we look at life (ourselves, others, and circumstances). Psychologists refer to it as "*shifting your paradigm.*" I call it simply "*changing your mind.*" Though the extent of programming acquired by the time one reaches this level of awareness should make change simple, it doesn't mean change will necessarily be easy.

Desire will always be the overriding motivation for change.

To shift your paradigm is to re-adjust your focus and the way you interpret life events. Change happens when you allow new information to override subconscious core beliefs such as prejudice, hatred, and other negative ideas that can cause you to miss so many wonderful GPSs. Let me illustrate how I found a GPS with a shift in my paradigm and a can of Planter's Peanuts.

Among my several professional designations, I'm a licensed realtor in an office of about forty agents. When I started there, everyone seemed very nice, except for this one man who would never speak, and who seemed sort of grumpy to me ("to me" being the operative). This went on for months. I would speak. He wouldn't. I was beginning to become quite annoyed with him because in my opinion his behavior was quite discourteous. My upbringing dictates that one return a greeting when a greeting is extended, and that when entering the occupied space of others, one extends greeting to those already present. Well, it both-e red me that he didn't like me (or so I thought) and I decided I was going to win this guy over by being my well-mannered, likeable self. I would give him a generous smile every time we crossed each other's path. I even began to greet him by name saying something like, "Hey there, Sid. It's a gorgeous day out there, isn't it?" Still, not a word did he utter. The next time he came into my work area, I said, "Hey there, Sid! Things going O.K. today?" And he nodded! "Well, Well, Well!" I said to myself. "I'm making progress."

About a week or so later, I was on the duty agent's desk with a canister of Planter's cocktail nuts when Sid came in. "Hey there, Sid!" I said. Without returning the greeting, he asked if a fax had come in for him. I got up to check and told him something was coming through, but I wasn't sure if it was the item he was looking for. He would have to wait or check back later. He waited.

This was the defining moment!

I said, "Here, have some peanuts," and before he could answer, I just started pouring some in his hand.

He said, "Thanks!"

I could hardly believe it! He's talking!

He apparently liked peanuts as much as I did, because he kept eating them and I kept pouring them. For the next few minutes we stood there chatting about his days as a fighter pilot, the trips he takes in his own airplane, and on and on and on! From that day forward, Sid has been one of the most delightful people I've had the privilege of knowing.

It turns out he is an extremely shy man, and over time I discovered that he is a caring, funny, smart, helpful, and interesting man. One of the nicest people I've ever met.

Who changed here?

Sid or me?

What changed?

Clearly, my mind about him.

We have a choice in how we view people and situations. Look at how much good time was lost because my negative paradigm deflected a negative interpretation onto Sid. None of what I thought about Sid was true. A conscious shift in my paradigm empowered me with a clean and healthy perspective that enabled me to get to know him, to understand him, and to make a good friend . . . *all because of a change of mind and a can of Planter's peanuts!* Just think how many GPSs you will find when you make the choice to shift your paradigm—to change the way you see the world, others, and yourself. How many relationships or circumstances will change for the better because of it?

CHANGE YOUR THINKING. CHANGE YOUR LIFE!

BELIEVE GOD

Another powerful premise that will reinforce your good fortune in finding GPS is one that certainly every true believer accepts without question.

GOD IS WHO HE SAYS HE IS AND
HE WILL DO WHAT HE SAID HE WILL DO.

That's right, folks! Either He is or He isn't. But you must decide. There comes a time when you must declare what you really believe about God. The question of whether He is or isn't must be put to rest once and for all. Either you believe He is who He said He is and that He will do what He said He will do . . . or YOU DON'T! It's that simple! There can't be any middle-of-the-road position on that. So, for the record let me state,

I BELIEVE HIM . . . MATTER SETTLED!

I believe Him because of what His Word says and because my own history confirms it. Because of all He has brought me through, I've learned I can trust Him implicitly. When I reached that point of spiritual maturity when I could recognize His sovereign hand in everything, pleasant or not, my paradigm began to shift *more away* from "the problem" and *more toward* the "problem solver."

From Genesis to Revelations, God repeatedly describes who He is and how much love and regard He has for us, the most unworthy of His creations. King David, being fully cognizant of this unworthiness, was so bewildered by God's care he wrote in Psalms 8:3-4, "When I consider thy heavens, the work of thy fingers, the moon and the stars . . . what is man, that thou art mindful of him? And the son of man, that thou carest for him?"

But for His Grace, even in times of trouble, the Lord enables me to recognize and experience blessings I would ordinarily miss because of my attempts to handle the situation my way rather than surrender it to Him. Blessings such as the strength He gives to get me through the day when I'm certain I won't make it until noon. Blessings such as the compassion He enables me to somehow muster up to comfort someone who's hurting despite my own emotional bankruptcy. Blessings such as the indescribable peace He gives me when the tempest is raging fiercely around me. His Word offers promise upon promise of His love and faithfulness.

We have to decide once and for all if we're going to trust Him or lean on our woefully inadequate understanding (Proverbs 3:5-6).

He gave His life for me!

My God, what more can He do?

GET SATAN FROM BEHIND YOU

When it comes to undermining our willingness to trust God, the emotions of fear, doubt, and worry are Satan's most prized weapons of choice. He knows that if he can cause us to look skeptically on the promises of God, our fate is sealed and defeat is certain. Instead of causing us to *run to* God, these emotions most often cause us to *retreat from* God—or at least to diminish our interaction with Him in prayer, worship, and Bible study leaving us wide open for his most vicious assaults.

Satan is the master manipulator. The horror images that loom across wide theatre screens these days in high-definition photography, though surreal (especially if you're sitting in the front row in a dark theatre), don't come close to his ability to animate, exaggerate, and escalate our fears and vulnerabilities. Zig Ziglar refers to this as **F.E.A.R.**:

FALSE EVIDENCE APPEARING REAL

Under that kind of simulation and intensity, it would be hard for even the Pope to find a great parking lot, let alone a great parking space! This kind of fear doesn't come from God (II Timothy 1:7), which is why it is so important that we understand how to identify satanic attacks and learn what we can do to combat them.

I'm reminded of a nature show I once watched on the Discovery Channel.

A pack of hyenas was attacking a wildebeest. Though large animals, a lone wildebeest stands absolutely no chance against the aggressive, invasive tactics of the predatory hyena. The wildebeest was running for its life with the hyenas in pursuit. As the chase persisted, the hyenas took turns leaping up on the back of the wildebeest and with their dagger-like teeth began biting into its hide. The wildebeest would manage to shake the hyena off, but another would leap on and take its place.

Finally exhausted by the running, the fighting, and what was imaginably excruciating pain from the bleeding gashes, the wildebeest began to drop slowly to the ground no longer able to put up any kind of resistance. The hyenas then closed in and literally ate the wildebeest alive.

I remember thinking, "Wow! That's exactly what worry does." It takes you beyond the point of exhaustion and slowly robs you of the strength needed to fight off the vicious attacks of Satan. It was when I was brutally assaulted by what seemed like the entire satanic militia that I came to understand what was happening to me and how I had to respond.

In the winter of 1991, having recently been totally defeated in a business venture I had undertaken, I was looking through the classifieds for an opportunity to make money FAST (morally and legally, of course). This meant commission sales. I had worked years before that way and made a lot of money, that is, until Operation Desert Storm put a halt to everybody's spending and sending the country into swift economic decline.

One very interesting ad caught my attention. I had seen it before but had skimmed right past it. Because my circumstances then, apparently, weren't as severe, I wasn't able to see it for the opportunity it was (which can often be the case when our needs are being met). Desperate circumstances have a way of shifting your paradigm. This time, I took notice.

The ad was for a commission sales counselor for a cemetery company that provided death care services to families before-the-need. "A cemetery," I thought. "Death care services? Pre-need? Yeah!" Talk about a product everybody is going to use! Economic decline or not, death was happening every moment, everyday, everywhere. "This is it!" I said. How could I possibly miss? If I did half as well as I had done selling luxury cars, something everybody wanted, I would make a killing (no pun intended) selling something people absolutely needed to have.

Although it was about six o'clock in the evening, I called the number listed in the ad on the chance someone would still be there. I was right. A gentleman answered and I began explaining my reason for calling and requested an interview. He was delighted and asked me when I'd like to come in. I said, "How 'bout now?" After a stunned pause, he said, "All right!" "I can be there by 6:30," I said. "Fine," He said. "I'll see you in a few minutes, then."

When I arrived, I met with the sales manager, who explained in detail the rationale and scope of their business. The commission plan was excellent and I could see this was just the kind of opportunity I needed to get my life back on track. He hired me on the spot, but said the next training class would begin in about three weeks. "Three weeks!" I'm thinking. There was no way I could wait for three weeks. My ship was sinking fast, and I needed to get started yesterday.

I explained to him that I knew how to sell. All I needed was an understanding of the product and knowledge of the approach. Whatever training required had to be accelerated. I needed to get started NOW! So, in lieu of waiting for a regular class he had me shadow his assistant manager. We went on a presentation that very night. The plan was for me to work with him for the next two weeks but I didn't see him for but a minute or two the whole time, and for about three months I worked on my own.

I cold-called. I knocked on doors, followed-up on leads, sent mailers; you name it, with not the first appointment. I employed every sales strategy I knew and was getting nowhere. What was I doing wrong? It was becoming clearer by the day that death-care planning just wasn't something people were jumping up and down to talk about no matter how practical it was.

One particular morning, I had gone out to cold-call on neighbors, but again with no success. After all that big talk about knowing how to sell and "fast training," I hadn't booked one solitary appointment or produced a single sale. Humiliated and discouraged, I gave up and went home. As soon as my key turned the lock and I stepped inside, I broke down and cried pitifully as I made my way up stairs to my room. Without even undressing, I lay back on the bed and fell into a deep sleep. This was around two 'o clock in the afternoon (highly unusual for one who typically can't sleep in the daytime).

The phone woke me. On the other end was my good friend Evangelist Julia Robinson, who along with her husband, Pastor Joseph Robinson, founder of the Royal Oak Pentecostal Church in Landover, Maryland. She said the Lord had moved upon her heart to inquire of me and wanted to know if I was all right. I couldn't even play it off.

I began to cry again as I shared with her exactly how I was doing. That was when she alerted me to the fact that I was under a vicious satanic attack the intensity of which indicated God had a mighty purpose to fulfill through me and Satan was desperate to thwart it. Everything I was experiencing, explained Sister Robinson—defeat, depression, humiliation, fear, doubt, worry, abandonment, even fatigue—were simply the tools he was using to cause me to "curse God and die (Job 2:9)." "You see, Margaret," she continued, "the question isn't 'What are you doing wrong?' Rather, 'What are you doing right that Satan would come at you with such a vengeance?'"

Sister Robinson prayed with me and ordered me to get up and get moving. She told me to turn on some upbeat Christian music and start praising God for everything I could think of.

It was now about five 'o clock in the evening and still light outside. I did exactly what she told me and headed out to resume calling on neighbors with a renewed confidence and peace. Around 6:30 p.m. that same day, I had made my first sale, and my subsequent success in that business for the next five and a half years was unprecedented.

GLORY TO GOD!

Satanic attacks can be brutal, ambushing you so quickly you don't have time to even process what is happening to you. But, Praise God, by the shed blood of Our Savior at Calvary, the Holy Spirit gives us the greatest tool possible with which to wage an unbeatable counteroffensive. Through Christ, we can keep Satan from getting behind us and in front where we can more readily see him.

PRAY CONTINUALLY

Prayer is the medium God designed to enable us to communicate purposefully with Him. It literally catapults you right into the Throne Room of Grace, which is accessible to believers everywhere all the time. Prayer is the opportunity to praise and thank God for who He is and what He does for us and through us. In a personal context, it is the privilege to go to Him in spirit and in complete truth, privately lying bare whatever we need from Him and whatever is on our hearts (Ephesians 6:18). In spiritual warfare, it is the most effective weapon we have at our disposal, which is why we are admonished to do it ceaselessly (I Thessalonians 5:17) both for ourselves and for each other.

**THERE IS NO GREATER POWER ON
THIS EARTH THAN PRAYER.**

While here on earth, Jesus was a praying Savior and when He prayed, marvelous things happened. In fact, Jesus relied so heavily on prayer that He would go off in the wee hours of the morning well before dawn and in the evening to have that precious private moment alone with The Father (Matthew 14: 23). Recognizing the power of prayer and witnessing Christ's discipline in the matter, the disciples implored the Lord to teach them how to pray (Luke 11:1). If the Son of God sought The Father in prayer on a daily basis, how absurd it is for us to think we can somehow do without it.

**"THE EFFECTUAL PRAYER OF A RIGHTEOUS MAN
AVAILETH MUCH." JAMES 5:16**

Although the Lord delights in our prayers, He didn't create prayer for Himself. He created it for us because of all the sustaining benefits it provides.

For one thing, prayer clarifies our perspective by refocusing our attention appropriately on God and away from our circumstances and ourselves. Prayer purges the heart and refreshes the mind, releasing anxiety as we acknowledge our complete and total dependence on Him. Through prayer we "cast our burdens" on Him, the only one who can sustain us, confident He will never let the righteous be forsaken (Psalms 55:22). And, it thwarts Satan whose only mission on earth is our utter destruction (I Peter 5:8).

SATAN CAN NEVER ATTACK US SUCCESSFULLY WHEN WE'RE HUMBLED BEFORE THE LORD IN PRAYER.

Some of the greatest blessings ever experienced— good health, contentment, assurance, and peace—often are the direct result of a strong and effective prayer life. Prayer is the antidote for all negative circumstances.

Rather than attempting to take Satan on by yourself in a battle you cannot win alone,

"CAST YOUR CARES UPON THE LORD FOR HE CARETH FOR YOU." *I PETER 5: 7*

Take your cares to the Lord in prayer and *leave* them there!

STOP! COUNT YOUR BLESSINGS
"REMEMBER HIS MARVELOUS WORKS THAT HE HATH DONE; HIS WONDERS, AND THE JUDGMENTS OF HIS MOUTH." *PSALMS 105:5*

Despite what I've said, if at anytime you feel you can't think of anything positive about the day or the circumstances you're living in, you need to stop whatever it is you're doing and start a "**For . . . That . . . Because . . . List**." Commonly referred to as "counting your blessings," this exercise is a guarded ritual I try to do every day, usually in the early morning hours or late in the evening. Because we are admonished to "count it all joy" (James 1:2), the "For . . . that . . . because . . . list" counts everything for good: every experience, every encounter, and every circumstance whether it appears good or not. The length of my list illustrates when I'm focused too much on myself and not enough on God. This way I can get back on track with my sight properly focused.

A "For . . . that . . . because . . . list" provides a *partial* record or journal of the different ways God demonstrated His love and mercy on a particular day. I say "partial" because the full extent of His loving kindness can't be known until we see the Lord in Heaven face-to-face. As you compile your journal you'll easily see His goodness showing up in ways you'd never thought about. Some, you will have forgotten about in the course of a few hours. Others were never even noticed.

Here's how it works. It's very simple.

At the beginning of each day (or at the end—whatever works), on a clean sheet of paper (I prefer the lined notebook type), I list whatever I can think of that was a blessing that day. Each entry begins with the word "for," "that," or "because."

I begin with my thanks, honor, and praise for the character of God—for who He is. Then, for what He's done, what He's doing, and what He's going to do in your life. I word it just like that. Then I reflect on the day from the moment my eyes opened until the moment I closed them at night. I search for even remote blessings, like being thankful the trash was picked up. There are times I'm totally amazed at what God has done.

Try it with me and be blessed.

Let your thoughts flow freely and list whatever comes to mind. I guarantee you'll make twenty to fifty entries in a matter of minutes and surprise yourself tremendously. Take about five minutes to list twenty blessings (if you can list more, great!) but, shoot for at least ten. So much will emerge as tangible proof of how blessed you are, and how good God is even on an ordinary day. Let's go:

I GIVE THE LORD THANKS, HONOR, AND PRAISE . . .

1. for _____

2. for _____

3. for _____

4. for _____

5. for _____

6. that _____

7. that _____

8. that _____

9. that _____

10. that _____

11. because_____

12. because_____

13. because_____

14. because_____

15. because_____

16. for _____

17. that _____

18. because_____

19. for _____

20. that _____

At first it may seem a challenge to list twenty blessings in such a short period of time. Some of you might struggle to get ten. It may be because you're not used to focusing on the less-realized ways you're blessed each and every day. I promise, the more you do it, the more you will begin to recognize blessings you'd previously overlooked nor thought to consider. Reaching twenty, even fifty, in ten to fifteen minutes then will pose little in the way of challenge. In fact, I challenge you to take on this exercise for a week. I assure you that withintwenty minutes you'll have a list of blessings 100 to 150+ long that'll look a lot like this:

I GIVE THE LORD THANKS, HONOR, AND PRAISE . . .

1. **for** who He is
2. for what He's done in my life
3. for what He's doing in my life
4. for what He's going to do in my life
5. **that** I'm His child and He knows me by name
6. **because** He woke me and my loved ones up this morning
7. because He's an on-time God
8. that His love is unconditional
9. for His abiding presence
10. because he lives!
11. because he is my source and strength
12. that I can trust Him implicitly
13. that He is faithful
14. because He alone is God
15. that He's always the same
16. for the power of His Word
17. for His tender mercies
18. for salvation through the Cross
19. for forgiving my sins
20. because He will never leave me or forsake me
21. for the people He put here to support and encourage me
22. for my pastor and church family
23. for the love and fellowship of the ladies in my Sunday school class
24. for the opportunity to praise His Holy Name

25. for His Amazing Grace
26. for His promises
27. for a good night's sleep
28. for neither giving nor receiving bad news
29. (or, for enabling me to handle it)
30. for a reasonable portion of health and strength
31. for people who love and care for me
32. that I love other people
33. because the line at the store was short
34. because I made it inside just before the storm
35. because I can hear
36. because I can speak
37. that I have my right mind
38. for His divine protection
39. that it's 11:00 p.m. and I know where my children are
40. that my flight departed and arrived on schedule
41. for a day without incident
42. for great weather
43. for nice clothes
44. for the flattering wink from a passer-by
45. for peace of mind
46. that the check really was in the mail today
47. that the car started
48. because I passed the____test
49. because it's my birthday
50. for safety on the highway
51. for the stranger who put quarters in my parking meter
52. for a break in the check-out line
53. because that emergency vehicle racing past wasn't going to my house

54. that I found my keys
55. for gently revealing my shortcomings
56. for enabling me to resist temptation
57. for making a way of escape
58. for the stranger who fixed my flat tire
59. that I had a usable spare
60. because I can work and earn a living
61. for providing the essentials of life
62. that others pray for me
63. for people I can confide in
64. that I'm not in my grave
65. that I'm not at the grave of a loved one
66. for discernment
67. because He supplies all my needs
68. that no weapon formed upon me shall prosper
69. for options and opportunities
70. for this beautiful world we live in
71. for beautiful life memories of happy times
72. for peace and joy in my life
73. for enabling me to meet my obligations
74. for positive interactions with others
75. for the pleasant thoughts of others
76. for the driver who let me cut in traffic
77. for the laughter of little children
78. that I live in a free country
79. that my heart and mind desires to walk in His Way
80. for a few good friends
81. that the repairs cost less than I thought
82. for the company of my pet cat Herbert
83. for wisdom

84. for the help of others
85. for private time alone with the Lord
86. for the tranquility of the early morning
87. that I can see His love everywhere
88. for a great cup of coffee
89. for guarding my tongue
90. because life is a wonderful thing
91. that I have no problem money won't solve
92. for the success of my children
93. for sustaining my mother, siblings, relatives, and friends
94 for sustaining and encouraging believers everywhere
95. for the business He sends my way
96. for just hearing the voice of my children
97. because the house is clean and pleasant
98. for the aroma of beautiful flowers
99. for hearing from a long lost friend
100. for a great vacation
101. for a good education
102. for a cool drink of water
103. that I look good
104. for the nice compliment
105. for the friendly greetings from neighbors
106. for Christian radio and TV
107. for the loving relationship between my children
108. for their positive relationships with others
109. for the sound of the two of them laughing together
110. that I was a help to someone
111. for the cooperation of others

112. for time spent with my family
113. for a glorious sunrise
114. for the serenity of beautiful scenery
115. for a day at the beach
116. for bringing me through troubling times
117. that I'm totally inadequate and fully dependent on Him
118. because I can do all things through Him according to His will
119. because the Lord has a purpose and a plan for my life
120. because He knows what He's doing
121. because He proves Himself time and time again
122. that He can make a way out of no way
123. because a relative/friend (name) is feeling better
124. for insurance
125. for a relaxing evening
126. for the trials and the not-so-good times
127. for clean comedy
128. for a good laugh
129. for Christian music
130. for the opportunity to encourage someone
131. for the strength to say "No" when necessary
132. for restraint
133. for the strength to do what must be done
134. because He guides my decisions
135. that I feel good about myself
136. for the smiles on my loved ones' faces
137. for children with integrity and good character
138. for their loving hugs
139. for their respect and devotion

140. that He is God all by Himself
141. for increasing my understanding
142. for increasing my faith
143. for rest in His love
144. for the increase in my earnings
145. for the opportunity I had hoped for
146. that I feel great today
147. that I can think, read, and write
148. for a car to drive
149. because I don't have a car payment
150. for a hot, steamy shower/bath
151. that I know Him for myself
152. that He hears and answers my prayers
153. for the sun shining on my face
154. for the old hymns my mother sings
155. because God is good all the time
156. that my cat Herbert came home this morning
157. for a great place to live
158. for the kindness of others
159. for the beauty in nature
160. for a majestic sunset
161. for silence
162. for rest and relaxation
163. for modern conveniences
164. that my children know the Lord for themselves
165. because my computer didn't crash
166. because Heaven is my home
167. that He loves me with an everlasting love
168. because my neighbor cut my grass
169. because Jesus is Lord of Lords
170. because one day I will see Him face-to-face

171. for a family of long-livers
172. for the new people I meet each day
173. for a strong military defending this country
174. for all those who preach the true gospel
175. for the pleasure in a good foot/back massage
176. for a pleasant picnic in the park
177. for a nice drive through the country-side
178. for the opportunity to travel
179. for the colorful changing of the seasons
180. because the technician serviced my car without charge
181. for my new in-laws
182. for a few dollars in the bank
183. that I may not be what I should be but, I'm better than I used to be
184. that I looked up in the nick of time to avoid an accident
185. that He saves me from myself
186. for the thoughtful gestures of others
187. for the ability to taste a home-cooked meal
188. for that cozy feeling sitting by the fireplace/campfire
189. because my team won
190. because I got the job/promotion/contract
191. that I arrived on time/late
192. that the heavens have not fallen
193. that God is still on the throne
194. for an unexpected gift
195. because someone thought about me
196. for the joy in reading a good book
197. for a good hair day

198. for the thrill in winning
199. because I got a great parking space
200. **because . . . I'M STILL HERE!**

I could go on and on!

Notice the gradual spiritual depth of my list. It increases as the length of the list increases. The deeper I dig, the more blessings I find. Some I'd never thought of before; others I'd simply forgotten. That's what makes this exercise so incredible. It enables you see that even on an *ordinary day*,

God is good!

In the future, when you start to indulge yourself in a pity party, stop for a minute and recall the past victories the Lord brought to you. Pull out a clean piece of paper and begin your "For . . . that . . . because . . . list" naming every good thing, despite whatever you may be going through. Use a cocktail napkin if that's all that's available. If you can't come up with anything on your own, use some of the items listed on mine.

Here is something else that has worked for me during those times I've felt sorry for myself or thought no one cared. Try re-reading old greeting cards as a way of reminding yourself of the affections of others. Cards, notes, and letters represent precious time and effort others have spent to show you love. In one of my closets I have a huge clear plastic zip-lock bag (I have no idea where it came from!) full of cards sent to me over the years. With each reading I get to relive those loving expressions and happy times and, for a moment, I'm removed from my present day cares. The sentiments expressed are as warm as a hug (always good medicine for whatever ails you!). They remind me of what matters most in this life and just how blessed I really am.

Should Satan's attacks overpower you to the point of despair, call on a good Christian friend like Sister Robinson to throw you a lifeline by praying with you. Begin a regime of daily Bible reading and commit to memory scriptures that will comfort and strengthen you. Tune into a Christian TV program or radio station (like *Family Radio* out of Oakland, California). Then, submit yourself *fully* to the Lord, who is worthy, and give Him praise for all He's done! Just think of the testimony you'll have to bless others with.

**This is the day the
Lord has made.
I will rejoice and
be glad in it!**

Psalm 118:24

TRUST AND FAITH
CHPTR8
♥ STATE OF JOY ♥

Go 'head . . . Make Your Own Parking Space!

How often have you attended an event and found difficulty parking? To compensate, some drivers drop their passengers off at the entrance, park a distance away, and walk or take a shuttle back to meet them. Others, having anticipated the parking problem, may leave their cars at home and use the Metro. Some may get upset and just leave. But others, rather than abandon the event they came to enjoy, may *create* their own parking space — on the lawn or wherever else — as long as they are able to participate.

Life is like that sometimes. I wish life was always like a lovely spring day — a sunny, warm, and clear day — when you could lie on a soft blanket and look up at the big blue sky without a care, feeling the gentle breeze pass through your hair and across your face. Yet, despite all the "hoping and awishing" (as my good friend Gracie would say), sometimes it seems as if you can't catch a break for anything. As they say, "Sometimes the dragon wins!"

Even on days that start out wonderful, by the end of the day, you still may be flanked with problems and troubles not even of your making. Some days, despite your best effort, it just won't be easy getting the great parking spaces. On days like that, consider yourself among the fortunate if you get a space at all! Other days, you might see a space but, getting it won't be easy because Murphy's Law is alive and well. You know, "What can go wrong will go wrong." That's when you have to improvise. Like Gladys Knight sings, "I really gotta use my imagination." On days like that, you have to get *really* inventive and create the circumstances that will bring about a blessing of some kind.

So when you don't like the way your day is shaping up and you can't see a GPS in sight . . . make your own parking space! Yes, sometimes you have to make your own day! As I've stated repeatedly, "Attitude, Attitude, Attitude!" The quality of your day — your very life — depends more on your attitude than on anything else. On those days,

> You gotta be bad. You gotta be bold.
> You gotta be wiser. You gotta be hard.
> You gotta be tough. You gotta be stronger.
> You gotta be cool. You gotta stay calm.
> You gotta stay together.
> All I know, all I know
> [Go 'head and make your day!]
> *"Gotta Be" by Des'ree*

Chuck Swindoll, president of the Dallas Theological Institute and the speaker for the "Insight For Living" radio ministry, explains the importance of attitude this way:

The longer I live, the more I realize the impact of attitude on life. Attitude, to me, is more important than fact, is more important than the past, than education, than money, than circumstances, than failures, than successes, than what other people think, or say, or do. It is more important than appearances, giftedness, or skill. It will make or break a company . . . a church . . . a home.

The remarkable thing is we have a choice every day regarding the attitude we will embrace for that day. We cannot change our past . . . we cannot change the fact that people will act in a certain way. We cannot change the inevitable. The only thing we can do is play on the one string we have, and that is our attitude.

I am convinced that life is ten percent what happens to me, and ninety percent of how I react to it. And, so it is with you . . . we are in charge of our attitude."

That pretty much sums up what's involved in making your own day. The *right* attitude — one predisposed to victory — will take you through most anything. And, the premise (assumption) *you adopt* about the day will determine the extent of beauty, peace, and satisfaction you experience.

Before the day gets started — even before you get out of bed — you should *decide* (choose) how you're going to react to life. You can't wait until Satan has you all tied up in knots. By then, it's too late.

One way to do it is by creating the right atmosphere and circumstances that you know will offer the best chance of guaranteeing a blessing in some way. Although there are many ways, here are fifteen (15) GPS inducers that help me make my own great parking spaces when it seems like that's the only way I'm going to get one.

INDUCER #1 CATCH A SUNRISE/SUNSET

I'm reminded of a beautiful song I've heard my mother sing for as long as I can remember. It is called "In The Garden" by C. Austin Miles. The first stanza reads: "I come to the garden alone, while the dew is still on the roses . . ."

I sincerely believe it is truly "when the dew is still on the roses" that one can find God Himself slowly strolling through this beautiful world He created hoping all the while some of us would join Him there. In the New Testament, a number of references are made to His daily ritual of rising well before dawn or going off somewhere in the evening to be alone in prayer and meditation with The Father.

I believe there is no finer backdrop on which to design a fantastic day than to begin and end each one in private meditation. One way I particularly enjoy these precious moments is in the magnificence of a sunrise or in the splendor of a sunset especially beside the water. For me, there is no greater catharsis for mind, body, and spirit so much so that David spoke of it continuously throughout the Psalms, particularly Psalm 23.

Despite the magnificent talents of all the Picassos, Da Vincis, and Van Goghs of the world — or even George Lucas for that matter with his sophisticated technographics — nothing man has ever done comes even close to the awesomeness of the lightshow God puts on in the heavens as He opens and closes out the day. No wonder Jesus sought The Father at those hours. He didn't want to miss the pageantry or the serenity that embraced their prayerful fellowship.

Private time with the Lord leaves you refreshed, energized, and hopeful. In it you can lay your burdens down, refuel your engine, and rest. Have you ever taken a stroll on the beach at sunrise? There's nothing like it. It will make all the difference in your day . . . your world . . . *your life!*

When was the last time you saw a sunrise or a sunset?

If it's been that long, you're forfeiting the greatest parking space there is — priceless time alone with The Father. Commit to getting up earlier to spend that time alone in prayer, meditation, and praise. You'll be less stressed and more productive as well as less agitated and more patient. To others you'll appear friendlier, more likeable, more cooperative, and helpful. Interestingly enough, you'll find others to be more so, too. In Psalm

46:10, He says, "Be still and know that I am God." In other words, *slow down!* Embrace the peace and beauty God sets before us every day in the people we meet and in the task we are called to do.

Inducer #2 Put on the Full Armor

"Life" is synonymous with "challenge." That's simply what life is: a series of perpetual, often unpredictable circumstances confronting us each day in its own unique way. Who can figure it? If you don't feel particularly challenged right now and life is everything you want it to be, I wouldn't get too cocky if I were you. Just wait a while. The greatest challenge of your life may well be lurking confidently around the very next corner.

Challenges may take a variety of forms: physical, spiritual, financial, or relational. We don't always know. Rest assured though. In whatever form they choose, they're coming, and they'll keep coming until the day your train to glory leaves the station. That's why no matter how fierce the rage of the storm or how calm the waters may appear, we must always keep our hand in the hand of the Man who stills that water and, with His Word alone, calm those roaring seas. You see,

**WE DON'T HAVE TO KNOW THE FUTURE.
WE JUST HAVE TO TRUST THE ONE WHO DOES.**

Everyday Satan is roaming about like a lion seeking someone he can devour (I Peter 5:8). The only way to withstand his sinister wiles is by putting on the Lord's full armor every single day (Ephesians 6:11-18). That necessary armor — salvation, love, faith, and truth — is found throughout the pages of the Bible, which is why the daily practice of reading scripture and meditation is essential. The heat of the battle is not the time to start getting dressed or to start sharpening your sword. Have your guns already cocked. Without them, you're a walking target for inevitable attack that could bring down an otherwise promising day.

Identify and commit to memory key verses that will anchor and empower you. The more verses you can commit to memory, the better prepared you'll be. When those fiery darts come flying towards you from every direction, anchor verses will come to mind when you're unable to think of any others. Anchor verses provide basic prayer coverage to every believer much like a driver is covered under an automobile insurance policy. The difference is prayer coverage is underwritten by Christ's Blood on Calvary. They were called "memory verses" in Sunday school when I was a kid. Thank God we all had to learn them. They've sustained me at my lowest points. To this day one of my most relied upon anchor verses is:

"TRUST IN THE LORD WITH ALL THINE HEART AND LEAN NOT UNTO THINE OWN UNDERSTANDING. IN ALL THY WAYS ACKNOWLEDGE HIM AND HE WILL DIRECT YOUR PATH." *PROVERBS 3:5-6*

When your memory arsenal is full of the Lord's promises, Satan has no chance of taking you completely down. Oh Yeah! He can rock your world all right but, he will flee when you rebuke him with the written word you recall from memory on a dime. Isn't that how the Lord handled Satan in the wilderness (Matthew 4: 4-1)?

"It is written."

"It is written."

"It is written."

Christ crushed Satan with the Word!

Inducer #3 Climb Out of Your Rut

I've heard a rut described as a coffin with both ends knocked out. That's no way to die, and even more certain, it's no way to live. The sad thing is many people are in that rut and don't even know it. Their lives are spent doing the same things they did yesterday, seldom adding anything new or scrapping what is no longer useful. They've been at it so long they can't make the distinction anymore. Life has become a treadmill of redundancy, predictability, and atrophy — a dull routine that can be changed but, only by change.

It's impossible to have a different outcome doing the same things.

So, what does your rut look like? Is it the hairdo you've worn since high school? The route you take to work? Your job? Have you acquired new friends, perhaps of a different persuasion? Or do you continue to surround yourself with the same kind of people with your same point of view? Have you rearranged the furniture lately? Taken a course in Chinese silk painting or ballroom dancing? Does your life now (or your wardrobe) look any different than it did five, ten, twenty or more years ago? If your answer reflects little to no change, I'd say you are in a serious rut.

Anyone who hasn't made much in the way of change is obviously someone who's intimidated by the prospect of doing something different. Radical change usually doesn't come quickly or easily, even when necessary. The deeper the rut, the more dramatic the change must be to create the greatest new possibilities. The important thing is to be open and flexible. Progressive little changes go a long way toward making a wonderful day and producing some incredible GPS.

INDUCER #4 DO WELL, LOOK GOOD!

When it comes to coping with failed relationships (something I've experienced a time or two), I always say, "The best revenge is doing well and looking good." The same applies when it comes to creating a good day:

DO WELL AND LOOK GOOD DOING IT!

This is especially true when life is beating you up and the dragon is winning. When I'm at my lowest, when I feel so defeated I just want to crawl into a hole and pull the hole in behind me, that's when I have to get up, clean up, and make-up because,

Looking bad doesn't help anything!

Over the years I've found that in times of difficulty (and definitely when things are going great), my appearance and the way I perform my duties may be the only things I can control. Though compliments from others are much appreciated (and welcomed), looking my best and performing well is something I do for *myself* because they are such powerful mediums for lifting my spirit and my confidence. No, they may not necessarily affect the outcome of any particular issue I may be facing. But, I sure do feel much better when I can look in that mirror and see a person I'm pleased with. How could God possibly be honored when we present ourselves to the world appearing as unkempt and uncared-for children? What kind of testimony is that for a God we say we trust? This may be a cliché but,

When you look good, you feel good!

And, when you feel good, you're powerful!

As difficult as it may be sometimes (and I know it gets hard), strive to look good no matter what. Drag yourself up and get moving. Take a shower. Brush your teeth and style your hair. Put on some make-up. Go to your closet and pull out the finest outfit you own (appropriate for the venue and occasion, of course). Take a deep breath, hold your stomach in, lift your head up, and pull your shoulders back. Strut like you have a million dollars even if you don't have a single penny. Look as though you're celebrating the greatest event of all times. You are ... *Today!* Hold it together in a dignified way as an expression of faith and trust.

NEVER WEAR YOUR PAIN ON YOUR FACE!

Rather, honor the Lord through your pain by looking good and doing your very best with what you have.

But, don't stop there. The same goes for your surroundings: your home, your office, and your car. Nothing makes my day more than when I open the front door after a long hard day and step into a clean house, smelling good, and peaceful. I recognized the effects of a beautiful environment on the mind and body years ago. However, passing that on to my kids when they were growing up was sometimes a real challenge. Thank God, they finally got it.

My home is an easy place to unwind and purge the cares of the day. The fact that the atmosphere is inviting and has a calming effect on the senses is no accident. Every item in it has a story. Though selected very deliberately, very few of the items were purchased at the same time. Great care was taken to see that everything harmonized. This is the essence of the Chinese practice of feng shui.

The condition of my house is an excellent barometer for my spiritual and emotional state of mind. When things are in disarray, it affects me in a negative way. I feel cranky and irritable. I'm not as sociable and I don't rest as well. I feel overwhelmed by what seems to be a magnified reflection of the disorder in my life. And, it compounds the stress I must already be under for things to have reached that point in the first place. I can't relax until order is restored.

For example, if my bed remains unmade for a couple

of days, it's no big deal. I'm probably just a little busy. But, it's quite another story when one side is piled so high with clothes, books, and magazines that you couldn't tell if I'm in the bed. If the floor hasn't been vacuumed for a while and the dishes are piling up in the sink; when a hundred pairs of shoes become an obstacle course to navigate in the dark just to get to the bathroom, I'm sliding fast. And, when I can't see my reflection in that pretty black Cadillac, I'm in a serious decline. For others, symptoms of the slide can be sleeping too much, constant fatigue, drinking, or drugs. That's when it's time to stop, snap out of it, and get things turned around beginning with self.

When your work area is clean and organized with everything properly in place, you get more done more efficiently than when you're buried under heaps of paper unable to find this, that, or the other. You look smarter and more confident and you feel more in control, which is its own reward. And, what a terrific feeling it is to drive along in your car after it has been waxed to the point where you can see yourself and the chrome wheels are shining like new money. Why even a hooptie cleaned up can make you feel like a million bucks after it's had a little TLC (it seems to run better, too!).

Take the time to get your surroundings in order. It goes a long way toward relaxing your mind by redirecting pent-up anxiety especially when you do it yourself. But, if you need to, get the kids to help or pay somebody. It's an investment in peace and sanity. The goal for each day is to get through *this* day, not tomorrow.

"TOMORROW WILL TAKE CARE OF ITSELF."
MATTHEW 6:34

Embrace the present moment concentrating only on what's within your power to control — *your reaction* to people and events that occur in your life. Go get your hair done. Get a manicure, or better yet, get a massage. Change the bed linen. Re-arrange the furniture. Paint a room. Besides taking your mind away from your troubles, you may acquire a new point of view and get a lot done in the process.

INDUCER #5 WATCH YOUR MOUTH

"FOR OUT OF THE ABUNDANCE OF THE HEART THE MOUTH SPEAKETH. . . . FOR BY THY WORDS THOU SHALT BE JUSTIFIED AND BY THY WORDS THOU SHALT BE CONDEMNED." MATTHEW 12:34-37

Some of the strongest admonitions in the Bible are about the tongue. Weighing only a mere two ounces or so, it has the power to exalt or to tear down; to hurt or to heal. The tongue has the power to topple kingdoms and destroy relationships. It is the most reliable instrument for revealing what's in the heart. To be sure, the Lord will hold us all accountable for how we use it.

God's positive words spoke an entire universe into existence. To a large extent, we have that same power by what we say, especially to ourselves. Our thoughts are the recorded conversations of the heart and the mind. What the heart says to the mind — good or evil — manifests in what we say. Whatever your heart conveys, so will be the nature of your thoughts and ultimately what will pass from your lips. What you say tells more about you than it does about the person or object under discussion. Chip Ingram, from the radio ministry "Living On The Edge," breaks it down this way:

- a gentle word reflects a tender heart
- a kind word reflects a loving heart
- a truthful word reflects an honest heart
- a song reflects a happy heart

While:

- a harsh word reflects an angry heart
- a negative word reflects a fearful heart
- a critical word reflects a bitter heart
- an over-reactive word reflects a restless, unsettled heart
- a filthy word reflects an impure heart
- a proud, boastful, or arrogant word reflects an insecure heart

The thought patterns we follow are learned behavior. All of us know people (and maybe ourselves) whose response to everything is in some way negative and counterproductive. Many people live their lives practicing the awful habit of gossip, criticizism, joking, sarcasm, insulting others, and using profanity. Because they've done it for so long, they themselves are often unaware that they are doing it, but everyone around them is. And, yet there are those who even in the worst of circumstances always seem to have a positive response to those same circumstances in the form of a compliment or a kind word of encouragement or comfort.

Because thought patterns are learned through the subconscious, they often prove difficult to unlearn. However, if the desire to do so is strong enough and conscious effort is consistently applied, change is possible. (Studies have shown that most habits can be broken in twenty-one consecutive days.) It's a choice.

FREEZE!

Try this two-part exercise. *Part One*: Answer this question:

IF YOUR THOUGHTS WERE BROADCAST OVER A PA SYSTEM, WOULD YOU BE PLEASED WITH WHAT OTHERS HEARD?

For the next few minutes, think about what you're thinking about. What are you thinking right now, at this very moment? What thoughts are running through your head?

- Are they good thoughts or evil thoughts?
- Are they motivating and complimentary or condemning and critical?
- Is this a "good hair day" or should everybody stay out of your way?
- Is there hope in your heart or are you waiting for the ax to drop?
- Are you a winner or a miserable loser?
- What are you saying to yourself, about yourself?

About others? Your circumstances?

When I did that brief exercise I quickly realized that even for a "positive" person like me, my thoughts seemed to drift *naturally* in a negative direction. I was amazed at how hard I had to work to keep them in a positive vein. That's because *negativity is natural.* We are born with a sinful nature. It is natural for us to have a propensity for the negative and the world around us reinforces it every day. That doesn't mean we have no choice in the matter. That's just it! We have a choice in this as in most matters. With conscious effort and desire we can do a lot to shift our focus toward the more honorable things in life.

Now, *Part Two*:

For the next twenty-four hours, begin to break away from the habit of thinking and speaking negatively. Refrain from verbally expressing negative thoughts of any kind for any reason. No cursing. No yelling at the wife or the kids for interrupting your football game. You can't "kiss off" the driver who cut you off in traffic or grunt at the cashier at the supermarket because she has to do a price check. Extend this exercise for the next 21 days or until the habit is broken, whichever is longer.

When you get up in the morning, when you get in your car, while on your break, on the ride home, before you go to bed, commit to speaking only words that help, heal, or cheer. Repeat the following at least once every hour to keep your thoughts in check:

"LET THE WORDS OF MY MOUTH AND THE MEDITATIONS OF MY HEART BE ACCEPTABLE IN THY SIGHT" PSALMS 19:14

Ask the Lord to help you with this. He alone is able, through salvation, to cut to the core of your *stinking thinking* — the need for a new heart. Begin to excuse yourself politely from people who engage in negative conversation. Oh yes, they're going to look at you a little funny at first. But, you'll begin to see others rise to your new standards and emulate your good example.

Finally, listen to your conversation and before you share your thoughts with anyone, ask yourself:

- Is what I'm about to say true?
- Is it necessary?
- Is it appropriately timed?
- Is it helpful and informative?
- Is it cloaked in kindness and love?
- Does it reflect love for Christ?
- Does it build good rapport?
- Will it inspire?

If the answer to any of these questions is "No," then *don't say it!* As Bill Sarvis, a good friend from my car-business days, used to say:

"THE LESS YOU SAY, THE LESS YOU'LL HAVE TO APOLOGIZE FOR."

Then there are "words" — powerful little mediums of imagery. The very sound of some words create powerful images that produce emotional reactions, some of which we're not even aware of. To prove it, repeat the following words in your mind and describe the images they induce:

peaceful	refreshing	delightful
solitude	joy	fun
calm	silence	rest
jolly	laughter	cheerful
tranquility	floating	serenity
love	blossom	springtime

How do they make you feel? What images came to mind?

What about these?

dark	dismal	gloom
depressed	tears	sadness
hopeless	somber	despair
frown	misery	winter
heavy	gray	fear

The very thought of these words probably evokes a negative reaction on your emotional well-being. Zig Ziglar makes this point well when he draws the hilarious distinction between a man's reference to his wife as a "vision" rather than a "sight." Words have implications. The things you say to yourself and to others shape not just your outlook but, also your destiny and their's.

WORDS PAINT YOUR WORLD.

To help make the best of every day, concentrate on words that enhance peace within yourself and harmony with others.

INDUCER #6 DON'T BE THE ONE WITH THE SAD STORY

Do you wear your heart on your sleeve? Have your friends or co-workers stopped asking, "How 'ya doing?" for fear you're really going to tell them? It's enough that things in your life may not be exactly as you would like them to be but, this too shall pass. Why make them worse by speaking negatively about your circumstances to anyone who will listen? Chances are they can't help (and often won't). I'm not suggesting that you not confide in a trusted friend or reach out for help when it's truly needed. We are supposed to share each other's burdens (see Galatians 6:2). But, don't always be the one with the sad story. Be mindful of the fact that you are not the only person going through a bad time. You're not the first and you won't be the last.

Everyone has their own load to carry regardless of how things may appear. Be careful not to overburden others with constant, senseless whining. It could add a weight on their shoulders they just don't need and cause you to miss the lesson your trial endeavors to teach you.

Besides, if you've put the matter in God's hands, what in the world are you still doing with it anyway? Make the best of the situation until it changes. Because, it will change.

Inducer #7 Take a Vacation

I know of nothing that can better cleanse the mind and restore the spirit than a great vacation. When I was a child, I used to think vacations were *optional* endeavors only for the leisurely self-indulgent. Of course, as I got older, I realized I was wrong. As a matter of fact, I think vacations are so essential that they should be mandated by an act of Congress. That's right. There should be an incentive of some kind--- a tax credit maybe--- to reward those who take time off to become better, more productive human beings. Think of how it would stir the economy. Everyone benefits, including business and society.

If you've never taken a *real* vacation, if you've never stopped the world and gotten off, you are not getting anywherenear the most out of what life has to offer. Quite the contrary. Life is getting much too much out of you! Even a computer needs to be shut down from time to time to purge itself in order to perform better. Don't people need the same kind of reprieve?

Everybody has his or her own concept of a real vacation. For me, it's the beach — Mexico, the Caribbean, Dewey Beach, Florida — any of a number of exotic places I've been blessed to visit in my life. I never tire of these places but, I can't just pack up and go whenever I want. I wish I could. (I'm working on it!)

One day it dawned on me: the same sun and sky above those exotic places is the exact same sun and sky over the beaches near my home. When I kick back and look up; and listen to the waves breaking over the rocks at Sandy Point; and smell the salty sea air, in those moments I could be anywhere in the world. This is one way that I satisfy my recurring need to unplug from the craziness by relying on the next best substitute available — my imagination. I began simulating real vacation experiences by taking "dream" vacations on a regular basis, at least once a week. No, they don't take me very far physically but, mentally and spiritually my dream vacations take me to another world.

When you dream, your mind doesn't know the difference. You can be anyone you want to be and go anywhere you want to go. I'll take a drive out to a local beach in the middle of the week when hardly anyone is there and I'll stay until the sun sets. It's the very reason I keep a beach chair, blanket, umbrella, straw hat, and cooler in the trunk of my car year-round. It is a great diversion.

Other times, I might take a drive through the mountains or through the green rolling hills of the countryside by myself or with select company. I pretend I'm a tourist in my own town. After all, there are a lot of interesting things to see and do but, as residents, we usually don't make the time unless we're playing "tour guide" for visitors. When my sister Ruth was in high school, she used the money she'd saved from her part-time job and booked a weekend at a luxury hotel just around the corner from our house. We'd pass by in the car on the way to the grocery store and see her lounging at poolside. She was on vacation!

It's wonderful doing things you usually don't do. Try leaving the car at home and taking the bus or the subway across town for lunch in an area you may not have explored before. It will give you a fresh perspective from a different vantage point.

To accommodate my little excursions, I recently bought a cute little combination picnic basket and beverage caddy for $2.00 at a flea market. What a find! The minute I saw it I thought, "This will be great to take on my next 'dream' vacation." Shortly thereafter, I was feeling stressed and I knew I needed a vacation in a desperate way. Not being in a position at the moment to trek to the islands, I simply made a nice lunch and took an afternoon "trip" for a couple of hours. I found a beautiful setting on the Potomac River only three miles from my house. This was in the middle of winter — with snow on the ground! There I was all wrapped up in my blanket (the one I keep in the trunk of my car), taking in beauty like I'd never seen before. Talk about reviving! It did wonders for my soul. In only a few minutes, I had been reborn!

If you can take a real vacation but, haven't for a while, by all means, please do so. You'll come back a new person. For those of you who may never have taken a real vacation or who can't right now, I fully understand. A "dream" vacation is an affordable and delightful stress-buster! It will refresh you and give you something interesting and exciting to talk about with others. There's no excuse not to.

Instead of complaining about what you don't have or

can't do or where you can't go (negativity *ad nauseam*), work with what you have. If the furthest you can travel is to your backyard, the rooftop, or under the boardwalk, with a little imagination you can still find a way to "vacation" there. If a few minutes is all you can spare, then lean back in your chair, prop your feet up, close your eyes, and relax. Let your thoughts drift to pleasant places. If the bathroom is your only retreat, then lock the door, light a few scented candles, and let Calgon take you away. That's a whole lot better than stressing to the point of burnout where you're no good to yourself or to anyone else.

INDUCER #8 LAUGH! - GPSS GUARANTEED

When was the last time you laughed? I mean, *really* laughed?

I'm not talking about a flip chuckle but, a cracking-up, doubled-over howl with tears-streaming-uncontrollably-down-your-face kind of laugh?

The same for a good healthy cry. When was the last time you cried so hard your body went limp as you fell quietly to sleep?

In either case, do you remember how you felt afterwards? Drained, but somehow refreshed?

As joy is to pain, laughter is to tears. Both are two sides of the same coin long recognized by physicians and mental health professionals for their powerful healing properties. Tremendously cathartic, they purge the body of stress and anxiety, invigorate the spirit, and add years to your life. Of the two, however,

LAUGHTER IS BY FAR THE BEST MEDICINE!

Whereas tears focus our emotions inward, laughter propels us outward. Laughter brings a fresh perspective to a situation and gives us power over even the most unfortunate of circumstances. Laughter enables us to rise above our suffering, loss, and pain. This doesn't diminish the importance of tears in any way because we also need to cry. It's just that at some point we must for our health's sake find a new perspective on the situation we are grieving over in order to move on. Laughter helps us do that. Tears don't. Picture this:

Some years ago, we used to have a little Daschund named Max. Max was a rescue pet and the sweetest little dog I've ever known, and we've had several. One summer, my kids went to Connecticut to visit our folks there. Max went with them. Somehow, someway, Max got out of the house and was later found dead in the street having been hit by a passing motorist. My kids were beside themselves, and when they called me at work to tell me what had happened, I was as devastated as they were. Max wasn't just our pet—he was family. He was even in our family portrait. Shucks! You call Max a dog, he'd give you that, "You talkin' to me?" expression. I went into the ladies' room and I cried and cried and cried. Even now tears are filling my eyes as I write this.

Later that afternoon, I called my sister Kathy, a psychologist, who listened patiently and tenderly as I tearfully recounted what had happened to Max. In an unhurried while, she began to express what I believe were her sincerest condolences for Max and acknowledged my obvious pain, but with an interesting disclaimer. She said, "I have to be honest with you. I don't know what on earth you're talking about!" And, after a momentary pause, we both burst out in hysterical laughter.

I love pets and anyone who loves them like I do could have empathized with my pain. But, Kathy isn't an animal-lover. She wouldn't hurt them or anything. She just doesn't want them around her. (She says if God wanted dogs to have a house, He would've shown them how to build one.) How ridiculous I must have sounded to someone like her who, although sympathetic, has no capacity for the level of affection I had for what she refers to as "just a dog." She simply couldn't relate.Despite Max's lack of value to Kathy, my family remembers him dearly to this day. He'll always hold a special place in our hearts. For a moment though, seeing the world through another person's eyes and the laughter it generated helped set my emotions on a proper keel and jump-started my healing.

With reality being what it is (often stranger than fiction), sometimes the only way to cope with it is to laugh. Any comedian will tell you that most of their jokes and funniest comedic material come straight from things happening to and around them every day (and they are not necessarily good things). Comedy is big business these days. It's big because so many of us are hurting and are willing to pay a premium for any antidote that will override our setbacks, difficulties, and disappointments. Laughter is a healthy antidote. We need to laugh!

So when emotions begin to run high and life gets a little too serious, try a laugh. If one isn't immediate, look for it. It's there! The world is a very funny place. For me, a call to my buddy Mark solves that. He's one of those naturally funny people who can say something or make an expression without intending to be funny and you're rolling on the floor.

Make it a point to be around people who laugh. Call to mind humorous incidents from the past — you know, something that never fails to crack you up whenever you think about it even though it may have happened years ago. But, if you haven't found a laugh or induced one by 11:00 p.m. (EST), turn to the Lifetime TV Network. Sophia Petrillo and *The Golden Girls* will take care of that — guaranteed! Whichever way it happens, whatever you have to do to make it happen,

GET IN A HEALTHY LAUGH EACH AND EVERY DAY!

It's one of my strongest prescriptions to attract all kinds of wonderful GPS and for an all-around wonderful life.

INDUCER #9 *MUSIC IN THE KEY TO LIFE*

There's an old saying, "Hum, and the devil will never know what you're thinking." A singing heart is a happy heart. Joy comes from the Lord. Since Satan can't infiltrate that joy, he surely isn't going to stick around and listen to it! He's going to flee as fast as he can taking his demons of worry, fear, and stress with him, which is exactly what you want him to do.

Aside from the music industry, which is continuously under fire for the type of music it promotes to young people, the influence of music on behavior has been well-understood for decades by TV executives, filmmakers, ad agencies, department stores, supermarkets, and elevator companies. Corporations spend millions of dollars each year for just the right music mix to draw customers in and slow them down enough to be subconsciously compelled to buy their products. It works like a charm, and they have the statistics (and the bucks) to prove it.

In today's fast-paced world of business, music plays a major role in creating less stressful work environments and better employee relations which translate into higher productivity. You'll never hear a drone in any of those places. But, make no mistake: although the music played in funeral homes may help bring comfort to the living and helps to establish reverent loving memories, the carefully selected tunes also help draw the family back to that establishment when services are needed in the future.

Whether you hum a tune, whistle, sing, listen to the radio, play an instrument, or play your favorite CD, the *right kind* of music can transcend your state of mind. There is music for every emotion that exists. If you're stressed, let the soothing strokes of a violin, piano, or harp penetrate the depths of your soul. If encouragement is what you need, put on Kurt Franklin or Shirley Caesar or Yolanda Adams. Any one of them will get you up out of your seat. And, when my heart is breaking or when I just need to feel God's loving assurance, there is nothing like the old hymns I've heard my mother sing over the years to rock me in the arms of the Savior leaving me with an incredible peace that surpasses all understanding.

As food is to the body, music is nourishment to the soul. The same can be said of colors and fragrances, which is why the field of aromatherapy and *feng shui* has abounded in western cultures, particularly in recent years. For centuries Asian cultures have understood how our moods and outlook can be manipulated by the subliminal effect scents and music have on the senses. When evil spirits overtook Saul, music from David's harp was the king's only relief (I Samuel 16:23). We need to be aware of the music we listen to and pay attention to the effect it has on our state of mind.

When it comes to making your day, get to know yourself at least as well as the strangers who design the subliminal systems in the marketplace. If today isn't one of your better ones, don't listen to sad songs or wear drab colors. Find a melody to reverse that mood. Choose music, colors, and fragrances to set the tone for the way you want your life to go. Their therapeutic properties will uplift your spirit, relax your mind, and reduce anxiety. I know people (my mother, for example) who are always quietly singing, whistling, or humming, especially when they are working. They do so to take their minds off their troubles or to cope with them. Soldiers in the military, workers in the field, even people on a chaingang typically set the cadence of their routine by a song or a chant.

Instead of becoming filled with "road-rage" when traffic is tied up in knots and it's a slow crawl going and coming, try listening to some good sounds and use the time to diffuse the stress of the day. Find the oldies station on your radio and enjoy the tunes that take you back to "the good old days." Sing out loud with the sounds of the 60's, 70's and 80's — the ones you know all the words to. For you chamber music types, let the soul-stirring beauty of a Beethoven, Chopin, or Mozart masterpiece vaporize the junk that infiltrated your head during the day. Of course, you can almost always count on the instrumental sound of smooth jazz to put you in a relaxing state of mind.

Music plays a vital role in the life of every society. It is a universal medium of communication and a mechanism to help you control your world. Identify the music that has the best effect on you and use it to set the tone of your life.

INDUCER #10 CHOOSE THE HILL YOU'RE WILLING TO DIE ON

Have you ever considered that it is possible to decide *in advance* how you're going to react to a situation? Well, you can. I do all the time. Every day is full of different scenarios and incredible surprises. That's life! Things happen! But, if you can embrace the idea that it is possible to respond to an unanticipated upset in a predetermined manner, you rarely will be caught off guard. This is called "prioritizing your upsets," and it will empower you to resolve effectively many issues before they even start. The military refers to this as "choosing the hill you're willing to die on."

Prioritizing your upsets simply means to decide in advance what's important and what's not in the grand scheme of things and attaching the appropriate level of significance to properly gauge your response. You're not willing to die for every cause or issue confronting you on any given day, are you? Of course not! Each potential disagreement, preference, or disappointment carries its own weight relative to the overall objective of making a wonderful day.

EVERYTHING ISN'T A 10!

Take my family, for instance. When everyone was living at home, one of the most important things to me was to create and maintain a warm and happy home life. I wanted home to be the favorite place for every one in the family, the place where we all felt valued and loved. But, there were moments when it wasn't always like that.

Though I knew before I even arrived home from work my son's room would be looking like a forty-mule team had run through it. I would start ranting and raving as if I expected something different. Preposterous! It's looked like that since he was born! But one day as I was going on and on with my now-usual harangue about how he kept his room, the Lord gave me a valuable lesson through the wisdom of my ten-year-old son. Darnley said: "What difference does it make?"

Surprised by his response, I paused for a moment to reflect on what he said and soon admitted he had a very valid point. In the grand scheme of things, what difference did it make?

Darnley was an exceptionally bright young man. He still is. He's always been funny, talented, and respectful to his parents and teachers. He got along well with his sister and was just an all-around, well-liked kid who never gave us a moment's trouble. There I was all over his case everyday about his clothes on the floor, his bed not being made—things that, honestly had nothing to do with anyone else but him. Considering all his other wonderful attributes, what was the big deal! I was the one making the proverbial mountain out of a mole hill and everyone's life miserable listening to my banter when in the grand scheme of things it was totally unimportant. How many more times was I going to die on that hill? From that moment on, I never bothered him again about his room.

So what? He wasn't a neat freak. But he is a great kid!

What difference did it make?

Absolutely NONE!

We agreed that as long as nothing was crawling around in there or emitting offensive odors he could live in his room (and his room only) any way he chose. (He did, however, have to agree to keep his door closed so I wouldn't have to see it and I agreed to not act surprised when I did.)

Who says you can't learn from your kids?

Since then I have taken the lesson and practice of choosing the hill I would die on into every setting I've experienced. There are very few hills I'm willing to die on nowadays because very few things upset me. I'm very clear on what's important to me and what's not. If it's not about my safety, my family, my principles or reputation, then, "Whatever!" That leaves me with a very short list of things that upset me. I don't take anything as seriously as I used to anymore and I'm a lot more flexible.

How does one establish the priority of potential upsets?

That's a very important question. I know of only one way — by surrendering control of your life to the Lord and asking Him every day to take control of your life. Life sometimes feels like a chess game with me as a pawn. But, God is indeed in control. Even though we may not understand the challenges we're faced with, we must still trust Him, believing ... "it is He that goeth with you, to fight for you against your enemies, to save you" (Deuteronomy 20: 4). So, just go with it. A fully surrendered life allows you to stand against whatever the day may bring.

"The battle isn't yours, it's the Lord's."
I Samuel 17:47

Inducer #11 Start Out Like You Can Hold Out

Time and energy is the most precious of all human commodities. It matters not if your name is Bill Clinton or Bill Gates, Oprah or Queen Noor, more of either is not for sale even to the highest of bidders. Twenty-four hours is the most any of us will ever get in any one day. Sometimes less, but never more. When it comes to managing those vital resources, my mother has always admonished me to be realistic. Like the hare in his race with the tortoise, begin the day with the end in mind. Approach every project or task in a logical sequential order and at a pace that will help you reach your desired outcome efficiently. In other words, "start out like you can hold out."

In creating the best life possible, you must be committed to creating the best day possible *everyday!* It makes no sense to start anything at a pace that will be impossible to sustain and ultimately undermine all your good intentions. Life doesn't just happen. With God's help, we have to make it happen! But, it can only happen one day at a time.

Most times when life goes awry, we're often our own worst enemy and is usually the one who deserves the credit when it is sabotaged. This can be for a couple of reasons. The first reason has to do with how we react to a situation. The second is because we often fail to distinguish between what really matters and what's of little consequence.

Making your own parking space usually doesn't just happen without involving some measure of planning. And, planning begins with recognizing your capacity to control to some extent the outcome of the twenty-four hours you have to work with. It is impossible to make plans of any kind without first having a goal and a clear sense of what is important in order to obtain it otherwise failure is certain. Many times our goals are impossible from the beginning and are often established without regard for our human limitations or the limitations of the day. A better approach is to establish the priorities of each day. Things change. Be realistic about what must be done and what can wait; what can be passed off to others, or eliminated altogether. At the end of the day, you'll have a greater sense of accomplishment which will result in greater satisfaction and less frustration. So much of the stress we experience in life is because we ignore this reality:

FAILING TO PRIORITIZE IS FAILING TO PLAN.
FAILING TO PLAN IS PLANNING TO FAIL.

To place among the leaders of the pack, runners in a race dress lightly to conserve energy as they sprint towards the finish line. Their goal is clear — to win! They've determined what's important and they don't burden themselves unnecessarily. It is by lightening their load and focusing attention only on what really matters that the race is won. Up until the day of the event they practice, work out at the gym, monitor their nutrition, rest, and attend to medical issues as necessary. Their plan to win is reinforced by the priorities they establish. If you begin the day feeling powerless with no control, you over-burden your mind with the notion that you're just a mere victim of circumstances and that life has somehow dealt you a bad hand. You have in effect planned a day plagued by feelings of defensiveness, hostility, paranoia, and defeat.

Again, YOL = YOC. Prophecy fulfilled!

It all comes back to attitude!

WE CREATE OUR OWN REALITY.

If you have a tendency to think this way, the first thing you need to do is make the decision to reverse your negative thoughts and predictions. Having a written "to do" list ordered by priority is extremely helpful when it comes to accomplishing the things that matter most. Even if everything on your list doesn't get done (which is often more likely than not), you'll be empowered by knowing that the most important items are taken care of. The rest ... well, that's what tomorrow is for. You will have at least accomplished something.

What's most important to you today? What is it that gets you up out of bed in the morning? Is it a desire to walk with the Lord? To show your family how much they mean to you? Maybe it's the work you do or the desire to please your boss? Whatever it is will be evident by the priority you give it, the amount of time and energy you dedicate to it, and the plans you formulate to bring it about.

PLAN YOUR GOOD DAY BY FIRST DECIDING TO HAVE ONE.

And, start out at a pace you can survive. Start out like you can hold out.

INDUCER #12 DON'T SET UP FOR A SETBACK

Naturally, there are circumstances that come about from time to time over which we have little or no control. However, there are many things we do ourselves that sabotage the promise of a wonderful day. To get the most out of living every day, it helps to be aware of the ways we sometimes undermine our own selves and create undesirable outcomes that could have possibly been avoided.

A *setback* can sometimes be a preventable scenario often created by a disregard for reality or a willingness to deny it. However, by being prepared and making the right decisions, circumstances can often be well within your ability to control. An example,would not be remembering to change the clocks at daylight savings time and avoid missing an important meeting or deadline.

A setback is a negative outcome or consequence that works *against* your best interest. It can cause you to feel paranoid or uncomfortable like tight shoes that hurt like the dickens, or a sliding undergarment. It's anything that distracts you and keeps you from being your best. Setbacks are something you simply don't need.

The best way to deal with a setback is to first acknowledge it then accept the reality of a an impending negative consequence should you not take appropriate action or make the necessary changes.

Take clothes, for instance. Rather than face embarrassment or suffer regret, my family would frequently ask each other's opinion about an outfit or accessory when we felt ambivalent, especially when a good impression needed to be made (*i.e.,* a job interview or a date). The question posed would be something like, "What do you think about this?" Or, "How does this look?" Our Rule of Thumb:

IF THERE'S DOUBT, THROW IT OUT!

Of course, the thoughts and opinions of the one asking prevailed. But, if something doesn't look right, feel right, or act right *to you*, regardless of what anyone else thinks; or, if you're simply not feeling it, don't even chance it. Take it off and choose it for the "absolutely-can't-miss-with-this-one" item, the one you know works.

It's your greatest assurance that a poor appearance will be one setback you won't ever have to worry about.

And, finally, when it comes to clothes and shoes especially, let me offer this piece of advice:

NEVER COMPROMISE COMFORT FOR STYLE. YOU'LL LIVE TO REGRET IT.

There are quite a few ways you can avoid setbacks that can get any day off to a bad start. For instance, if you have an 8:30 a.m. meeting in Baltimore and it's 7:45 and you're stuck in traffic in Washington, D.C., you're obviously not going to make it on time. Rather than deny that reality, *give it up!* Call ahead to let your party know. It will at least take the pressure off. When you finally do arrive, you can walk in unhurriedly and without compromising your self-respect by giving the old "flat tire" story to cover up for the fact that you simply got started too late. (Besides, everyone knows the truth anyway, particularly if it happens often!)

Few things create greater potential for a setback than having nature call when you're stuck in traffic or in the middle of an important meeting. Either scenario could ruin your whole day. Before either happen, take that little trip to the bathroom if you must, even if you are late. Similarly, it's also a good idea to fill your gas tank up in the evening instead of waiting until morning when the lines are usually the longest. This is a prime set-up for an unnecessary setback of panic and delay since you probably hadn't noticed you were sitting on "E" until you were in the driver's seat.

Nevertheless, if you have to go, you have to go. You

have no choice and you'll have no peace until you do. And, don't you even think about trying to make it in and risk running out of gas or getting stuck where there is no bathroom making matters worse. In the future, accept the reality of your physical limitations and provide for them. You'll be less self-conscious, more relaxed, and ready for anything.

INDUCER #13 TAKE CARE OF YOURSELF

Dr. Charles Stanley, president of the In Touch teaching ministry in Atlanta, Georgia, often refers to the acronym **HALT** in his messages.

NEVER GET. . . . TOO **HUNGRY**

TOO **ANGRY**

TOO **LONELY**

OR TOO **TIRED**

If we don't take care, the presence of either malady in the acronym could be symptomatic of a lack of trust in God. Instead of relying on Him to see us through these periods of vulnerability, we try to walk in our own strength, which is something a child of God simply isn't equipped to do. Failing to HALT may also represent poor stewardship of the temple in which the Holy Spirit dwells.

There is nothing more beneficial to the body and spirit as a good night's sleep especially when trouble is on the horizon. A good night's sleep will restore your soul and you'll often awaken with a fresh new perspective. After creating the world, God himself rested and He commands us to do the same. And, because He never slumbers or sleeps (Psalms 121:3-4), why in the world should

I stay awake pacing the floor and wringing my hands? If there were something I could've done about the situation with a crisis looming, would I've not have done it by now? Of course, I would've! When there is nothing you can do (Psalms 11:3), when you're faced with a situation far too big for you alone, go to sleep anyway.

GOD HAS IT ALL UNDER CONTROL. THERE'S NO NEED FOR BOTH OF YOU TO BE AWAKE.

It is also important to get some physical exercise on a daily basis. Exercise is extremely beneficial in reducing stress and anxiety, improving blood circulation and respiration, and weight control. And, contrary to popular belief, exercise actually reduces fatigue and hunger.

So when you're tired, burned-out, or just fed up, get out and do something. Take a walk around the block. Go work out in the gym. Run, ride your bike, walk, or rollerblade like I do. What you do doesn't matter as long as you get your heart beating strong and your lungs get a good work out. You'll feel better, look better, and you'll sleep better! With all the craziness in life that you can't control, exercise leaves you knowing there is something you can control — your body. (The other, of course, is your attitude.) Take good care of your body. You're going to need it. It's the vehicle that is going to propel you through the next half century or beyond.

Finally, be sure to get regular medical checkups, especially as you get older. Many of the advanced diseases and conditions physicians see today in many cases can be prevented or, at least, treated and managed if discovered soon enough. A good friend and an aunt are both ill this very day because they were in denial for years about serious medical problems they hadn't told anyone about, not even their doctors. Not only was the technology available for successful treatment early on, my friend is the widow of an Army veteran and my aunt (who up until she became ill) worked forty-five years in a hospital. And, both had superb medical coverage available. Go figure! Seeing what each is going through now, I can say without a doubt:

PREVENTION IS FAR BETTER THAN THE BEST CURE OUT THERE!

What you don't know, or won't admit, may kill you! So get those checkups! Use that insurance. You're paying for it, after all.

INDUCER #14 KEEP A SHORT ACCOUNT WITH GOD AND MAN

There is someone you need to apologize to. Whomever instantly popped into your mind when you read that opener is the one you need to get things right with. And, you know you do. How many more years of love and sharing are you willing to forfeit? How many more relationships will you let slip away because you don't have the courage and strength of character to offer them a sincere apology to make things right?

Well, it's time — time you swallowed your pride and say without compromise:

"I WAS WRONG. WILL YOU FORGIVE ME?"

These seven tiny words must be the hardest words in the English language to say because so many people seem all too willing to sacrifice generations of family, friends — anyone and anything — to keep from having to say them. How pathetic! How sad! God only knows what the possibilities would've been if egos had been set aside and people, even professing Christians, did what they know in their hearts to be right. The GPSs that could've been enjoyed are most assuredly too numerous to tally.

No one can enjoy true inner peace until they are honest with themselves and take responsibility for their actions in life. Those who think otherwise deceive themselves because not one of us can escape the abiding feelings of guilt and private shame experienced after having hurt or offended someone who didn't deserve to be hurt or offended; when we've wronged another child of God. You do whatever you can to suppress it but, it never really goes away. The silent guilt can be overbearing. I know because even now — forty or more years later — I am occasionally haunted by the image of a little girl I beat up without provocation one day when I was about ten years old only because I could. We were the same age but, I was bigger.

You'll notice I haven't mentioned her name. That's because I've forgotten it. But, what I will never forget is her sad expression and the sound of her whimpering as she crossed Jefferson Avenue and went home betrayed by her "friend." If I could see her today I would tell her how sorry I am for having mistreated her. She didn't deserve that. No one does. God only knows the impact that incident has had in shaping her life, particularly her attitude when it comes to issues of trust. It certainly couldn't have helped.

We need always to keep a short account with the Lord and others. That means purging ourselves daily through prayer and confession. And, not just for others, but for ourselves as well. Proverbs 28:13 says, "He that covereth his sins shall not prosper; but whosoever confesseth and forsaketh them shall find mercy." Everybody makes mistakes and sometimes acts in poor judgment and on ill motives. Unfortunately, that's what mortals do. But, it shouldn't be our lifestyle. "If we would acknowledge our transgressions and ask God for forgiveness, He is faithful and just to forgive us and cleanse us of all unrighteousness" (I John 1:9). And, so will most others we've wronged in life if we would only come clean and ask them to. Experiencing the joy of forgiveness is a wonderful GPS.

Per chance, Reader, if that little girl is you, please know that I know I was so wrong and I am more sorry than words could say for what I did to you. Can you ever find it in your heart to forgive me?

Should your apology be rejected, which is always a possibility, at least you'll have the peace in knowing you made the effort. Beyond that, it's no longer your issue. It's their's and God's. Just add them to your prayer list.

Inducer #15 Live with Integrity

A lawyer friend of mine told me about an anonymous client of his to whom he referred as the best client he ever had in the twenty-five years of his practice. Obviously a very special individual, I asked my friend why. What was it that made that client so special? He said almost every time he took on a client and conducted his investigation of the facts as told to him, the findings would invariably reveal that the client had either lied outright or embellished testimony thus calling the client's integrity into question and weakening my friend's capacity to build as strong a case as possible.

Conversely, the case presented on behalf of the favored client was highly successful. The reasons: the client simply told the truth and the opposition, despite their best effort, was unable to impeach this client's character. As clichéd as it may sound,

HONESTY REALLY IS THE BEST POLICY.

Seldom does regret follow a truthful response. And, the truth isn't threatened by repetition. The story can be told the same exact way time and time again.

An uncompromised life of honesty, integrity and fairness will exonerate most individuals in circumstances in which character will be the basis of the final outcome. At the very least, they might be afforded the benefit of the doubt. But, to compromise one's integrity is a two-edged sword. Not only is it a set-up for disaster, it can also be a most unfortunate setback with irreversible consequences lasting a lifetime.

A lack of integrity causes you to have to always look over your shoulder. It undermines the confidence to look straight in the mirror and be pleased with the person looking back at you. Lack of integrity compromises character and fosters distrust because we judge the motivations of others by the secret truths we know about ourselves: that is, liars believe they're always being lied to; cheaters believe they're always being cheated.

A life compromised by a lack of integrity will be a life overshadowed by duplicity and insecurity. Dishonest people know they're dishonest. And, because they are masters of hiding this fact so well, they cause untold hurt and sometimes ruin to innocent people who fail to perceive their motivations. Just think of the GPSs dishonest people could be enjoying by allowing themselves to be open, honest, and sincere when dealing with others.

The virtue of integrity will never be a set-up or a setback to the one who incorporates it into his character. To quote a verse I've heard my mother repeat for as long as I can remember and one that I totally embrace on my own:

"A good name is better chosen than great riches." *Proverbs 22:1*

Or, in the words of George Washington, our first president:

"I hope that I shall possess firmness and virtue enough to maintain what I consider the most enviable of all titles—the character of an honest [woman]."

**Commit random
acts of kindness**

Anonymous

TRUST AND FAITH
CHPTR9
♥ STATE OF JOY ♥

Make Someone Else a Great Parking Space!

The spirit of kindness is one of the most endearing qualities a person can possess and express toward another. The connotation of the word cuts to the core of the needs basic to every living soul: respect, compassion, acceptance, and gentleness. Our Lord and Savior Jesus Christ is the personification of this virtue which he demonstrated as He fed the hungry, healed the sick, and forgave the sins of the depraved. Kindness is second in the list of sacred virtues in Paul's description of the word *love* itself (I Corinthians 13: 4).

Kindness can put a smile on the face of the sick, even the dying. It can cheer the lonely and encourage the needy. The acts of kindness we show toward others and those received from others are mediums through which blessings come.

173

About twenty years ago, we lived in a small townhouse community where one of our neighbors was a Hispanic woman of about seventy years or so. I called her "Señora." Both of us had dogs: ours was a Cocker Spaniel named Sherlock; hers a little Schnauzer she called Sebastian. Each morning the two of us would invariably meet as we walked our pets around the perimeter of the grounds.

Having anticipated their encounter, the dogs would begin barking with excitement as they approached each other. Both dogs would tug on their leashes, almost dragging us along in the attempt to reach the other. When they finally made contact, their tails would wag frantically as they kissed and sniffed and greeted each other the way dogs do. It was clear they were buddies. They were happy to see each other.

In much the same spirit (except for a few notable practices), the Señora and I anticipated each other's encounter as well. I could see her brilliant smile and the twinkle in her eyes from a distance, and I know she could see mine. When we reached each other we would hug, give each other a kiss on the cheek, lock arms, and walk the grounds as our dogs played and explored.

My family and the Señora have long since moved from that neighborhood, but I will on occasions run into her at the supermarket or a local restaurant, usually in the company of a family member. She's in her late eighties now and has become somewhat frail over time. But, the moment we see each other, we break into an ear-to-ear grin, hug, and kiss the other on the cheek just as we used to back in the day. The family member escorting her (seemingly always someone different) protectively looks on with that "Who is this?" expression but after a moment, quickly offers an approving smile because it is clear the Señora and I have the fondest affection for each other.

Like our dogs Sherlock and Sebastian, both of whom are gone now, it is a happy occasion whenever the Señora and I see each other. And, what's most remarkable about our acquaintance, which extends now over two decades, is that she can't speak a word of English and I can't speak a word of Spanish! But,

WHEN LOVE TOUCHES YOU, YOU KNOW IT!

When you're kind to others, others are usually kind to you. People will do all kinds of nice things for you when they perceive a kindness in your heart toward them. Although it is God who ultimately manufactures all blessings, those blessings will most likely be delivered through the kind acts of others. It's the reason why it's so important to be kind to everyone, even to strangers because,

YOU MAY NEVER KNOW THROUGH WHOM YOUR BLESSING WILL COME.

One Sunday afternoon in early winter when it was still warm enough to go rollerblading, I took off from my usual spot at the marina and went skating down the George Washington Parkway. About halfway back on the return trip, a young man with long blonde dreadlocks skated pass me headed in the direction opposite from which I had just come. In an exchange of about two seconds, we smiled, said "Hi!," and kept going. With the marina again in sight, I began preparing for my finish. I broke my speed down to a slow coast, unbuckled my helmet and pads, and unpinned my car door key from my sweater. With a deep sigh of relief I reached my car, exhausted but grateful that the eight-mile trek was over and I could finally sit down and take in the beauty of the river I love so much.

I pushed the key in the trunk lock to open it but nothing happened. I looked it over. It seemed like the right key so I tried again. Nothing. That's when I realized it wasn't the right key. It was the key to my car. I had my son's car.

Darnley was out of the country. When he's gone like that, he will park in my driveway and once or twice a week, I will drive it a short distance to maintain its good running condition. That's what I had done that day. The key to his car and mine look the same because they're made by the same manufacturer. I had inadvertently taken the key off the wrong ring so the key I was using to open his trunk with was the key to my car. His keys were in his trunk where I put them along with my things before I shoved off to skate.

I thought of calling someone, but who? For what? I had the spare key and Darnley had the other, so there would've been nothing anyone could do. "Ok, then I'll call a locksmith," I thought, who can either jimmy it open or, at worse, make another key.

And, where was my cell phone?

You guessed it — in the trunk!

What began as a leisurely afternoon was slowly slipping into a nightmare. As I said, it was winter, which meant daylight was swiftly drawing to an end and it was beginning to get cold and dark.

I decided to skate up to the marina office where there was an attendant still on duty. I explained my situation and asked if I could use his phone to call for roadside assistance, which I did not have the number for! I noticed he had a computer so I asked him if I could use it to access the service company on-line. He agreed and stepped out for a little while.

Great!

Unfortunately, this was not to be either as I didn't have my glasses (guess where they were!) and couldn't see well enough to read the screen.

Meanwhile, the attendant returned with a jimmy he had gotten from somewhere and with my permission attempted to open the car door but without success. He explained that he was having trouble because the car had power locks, but his friend Chip was really good at it. The only thing is Chris had gone and the attendant wasn't sure if he would be coming back today. Because that seemed to be a hopeless alternative, I reluctantly decided that the only solution was to try and guide the attendant through the process of signing on-line under my pin number to reach roadside assistance.

We had just gotten started when the attendant had to leave to handle a matter on the other side of the marina. When he returned, he said Chip was back and had gone to see what he could do about getting the door open. A few minutes later, I saw Darnley's car drive up to the marina office. A young man jumped out and said, "Ma'am, your car is open now!"

And, just who do you think the young man was?

The same young man with the long blonde dreadlocks who passed me skating on the parkway!

I thanked him profusely and, of course, I offered to pay him, but he refused. Insisting that he let me show my gratitude in some way, he finally acquiesced. "OK, then," he said. "How about some chocolate chip cookies!"

I went right home and made a batch of the best chocolate cookies ever for him and his friend in the office.

The Savior admonishes us to,

"BE NOT FORGETFUL TO ENTERTAIN STRANGERS: FOR THEREBY SOME HAVE ENTERTAINED ANGELS UNAWARES." *HEBREWS 13:2*

Thanks, again, Chip! You truly are an angel!

SMILE!

A warm, sincere smile is universal and has the same meaning virtually anywhere on the planet. That's probably because humans are the only beings in God's creation that can smile. (We're also the only ones that can laugh, cry, and frown!) When the spoken word fails or is for whatever reason unavailable, a smile will most always be unmistakably understood. A smile can project a powerful message of goodwill and genuine concern whether the gesture is extended individually or in combination with others gestures such as a hug or nonsexual touch.

When you smile, most people instinctively smile back.

Try it right now!

Look at someone whether you know them or not and give them a nice smile.

They smiled back, didn't they?

Of course they did!

A REAL SMILE IS HARD TO RESIST.

The way a bulb lights up a room, a smile lights up the heart of whoever is the recipient of it. My smile is brilliant. I consider it among my greatest attributes in all personal encounters and is a feature I am well known for. In fact, I smile so much I tell people that it's not a smile, it's just the way my face it shaped. It keeps my dentist paid, too!

A "real" smile engages the entire face, especially the eyes, while simultaneously showcasing the teeth in an ear-to-ear grin — not the closed-mouthed, tight-lipped empty contortions usually accompanying a shifty-eyed attempt at avoidance. One sure way to know it's genuine is by the length of time it lingers.

A REAL SMILE IS IN THE EYES AND FROM THE HEART.

While being prepped recently for a non-emergency

procedure at a local hospital, I could see the smile in the eyes of every practitioner that entered the room as I lay there on the gurney even though the mask they all wore concealed their noses and mouths. Though the procedure was pretty much routine, their smiling eyes and reassuring tones of voice added greatly to my comfort.

Have you ever noticed how impossible it is to frown and smile at the same time?

Try it.

You can't do it, can you?

Everyone in business knows (or should know) how important it is to greet customers with a smile and to project a cheerful disposition when speaking with callers on the telephone. Having spent a considerable amount of my career in commission sales, I, for one, surely recognize the imperative of making the best first-impression possible to create within my customer the desire to do business with me. In my office, I kept a mirror hanging on the wall in front of me so I could see myself as I spoke with callers on the phone. When I picked the receiver up (by the second ring), it was show time! Whoever was on the other end got my biggest grin and most pleasant greeting. Believe me, if a smile is in your voice, they'll hear it. If it's not, it can hit you in your pocketbook bigtime.

A SMILE CAN MAKE ANYBODY LIKEABLE.

And, they're free!

Like a smile, a caring, nonsexual embrace or touch on the hand, shoulder, or upper back have extremely satisfying emotional properties that benefit both the receiver and the giver alike. I'm a hugger. I may hug someone I've just met, depending on the situation, and if I perceive the person to be receptive. It is an extremely effective bonding mechanism that has worked well for me throughout my personal life and in my career.

When offered properly, a hug will transform a stranger into a friend and is a lot more personal than the usual handshake. If at the beginning of an encounter I perceive the person might not be receptive, I'll instead step closely towards them and offer a hearty handshake with one hand, while lightly laying my other hand on top of theirs. After a brief exchange and a little time spent together, they're most always receptive to a hug at the end. (Largely a function of my naturally outgoing charm and charisma!) Actually, I don't recall a single occasion where the person took offense at such expression. Quite the contrary. It seems that people want a hug, especially women. They seem to need it and are grateful when they receive one. Just use your best judgment.

A sincere smile, a proper touch, or a comforting embrace provide the psychological validation we all need in life because these gestures communicate value and caring. These expressions have the power to lift the spirit and help usher people through difficult situations, relieving stress and anxiety, even if only for a moment. And, although they may not necessarily change the circumstances, they can provide encouragement to uplift ones outlook to formulate a proper response.

GIVE AN UNEXPECTED GIFT

This is a "can't-miss."

Do you really want to make your own day?

Do you want to find the greatest parking spaces in the world?

Then try making someone else's day. Give them a gift they weren't expecting, but don't just *give* it to them. Make it an anonymous surprise. Wrap it up in pretty paper and bows, then stand back in a secret place and watch them open it. (Even now, can't you feel the excitement and a wonderful anticipation building in your own heart?) When they finally unravel all the trimmings, the joy that overtakes them will bring tears to your eyes and to their's, too, as they exclaim, *"You've made my day!"* They'll never stop talking about it. I'm not sure who is more blessed — the giver or the receiver. I actually think both.

Don't get me wrong — random acts of kindness are not about buying a lot of gifts and passing them around like Santa Claus. Rather, it's about the need to feel cared for in ways money can't buy. And, it's about being willing to sacrifice, when necessary, to show each other love.

By now you know I've got two great kids that I'm absolutely crazy about. I thank the Lord for them because they have taught me so much about loving. They're both very good at it.

In September a few years ago, Darnley and I were walking through a department store shopping.

As we moved through the store, we passed a display of Japanese fishbowls on which I made a fleeting remark about how beautiful they were while never even breaking my stride. We continued in the direction of whatever we were there for, made our purchase, and left the store.

The next morning, leaving for work as I normally did, I headed toward the driveway where my car was parked. Through the window I could see something was on the driver's seat, but I couldn't see what it was. When I opened the door my eyes bucked, my mouth flew open and I inhaled what seemed like a pound of air. I looked towards Darnley's bedroom window, which was over the garage, and there he was watching, waiting to see my reaction when I found the beautiful fishbowl he had bought me — the same one I had seen in the store. Sometime during the evening he had gone back to the store to do this wonderful thing. I was overjoyed!

It was my birthday!

The beauty of this gesture wasn't the gift alone. It was the idea that he loved me enough to do something that special for me; something he knew would make my day — and he surely did!

You've surely heard the old adage, "What goes around, comes around." Well, that being the case (and I'm inclined to believe it is), wouldn't you think we would be busily sending around as many acts of kindness as possible, random or otherwise, so that the love they express boomerangs back to us?

Beverly and I were having dinner one evening at a 50's style diner in our area. It was our first time there. As the waiter led us to our seats, we noticed the little jukeboxes stationed at all the tables. As soon as he took our order, we began flipping through ours to find some old favorites. (I don't know if I mentioned it, but both my kids are musicians. They know those old tunes better than I do and they're half my age!) When I saw Sam Cooke's "You Send Me" among the listings, I put my quarter in right away and floated on his velvety voice right through dinner. As a matter of face, I fed quarters continually to hear it over and over until the time we left.

Weeks later, I was relaxing in our family room watching something on TV when Beverly bolted through the front door all excited, asking, "Where's Mom? Where's Mom?" I could hear her coming towards the room spewing, "Mom, I found it! I found it!" as she reached down inside her shopping bag. (I had absolutely no idea what she was talking about or looking for.) Out she came with a Sam Cooke CD with "You Send Me" on it. She said, "Mom, I know how much you like that song, and I've been looking for the CD for three weeks, ever since we were at the diner. Everybody had the cassette, but I wanted to get you the CD so you can easily play it over and over as much as you like."

On a six-hour trip the following week, it was Sam and I. From D.C. to Connecticut, I played one tune. Which do you think it was? Tough guess, huh?

At home, we share almost everything. When one of us get up for a glass of juice or something for ourselves, most times we get one for everybody. Should we forget, Beverly would say, "So ... just thinking about yourself, huh?" to remind us to be thoughtful of each other.

LOVE IS SACRIFICE.

It is impossible to look in two directions at the same time. When you focus your attention on the needs of others, you take the focus off of your own. In doing so, you'll find the strength you need to cope through virtually any circumstance.

BY MAKING SOMEONE ELSE'S DAY, YOU MAKE YOUR OWN.

Don't believe me? Try any of these acts of kindness and see.

- Cut your elderly or sick neighbor's grass when you cut yours. Shovel their sidewalks after the snow and clean off their car.
- Do other nice things for the elderly and sick, such as prepare a meal, wash their car, do their laundry, run errands, shop for groceries, do minor repairs, check in on them on a regular basis. (Every Sunday, my sister Irene visits women in nursing homes to give them manicures and do their hair.)
- Take a book to read to residents in your local nursing home.
- Take your well-mannered pet with you.
- Take a pitcher of a cool drink or hot coffee out to construction workers near your house.
- Call an old, old friend out of the blue.

- Send a handwritten note of love and encouragement to someone who needs it.
- Put some money in the expired meter of the car parked near you. ("Who's car?" you ask. I don't know, but they'll surely appreciate you for it!)
- Pay the toll for the next three cars behind you.
- Give the other guy the right-of-way.
- Bake your favorite dish for your colleagues.
- Purchase a meal and sit down and eat with a homeless person.
- Spend some quality time with an underprivileged child.
- Start a conversation with someone who appears to be sad or lonely.
- Adopt a single-parent family.
- Adopt a family from a foreign land.
- Lend an ear to someone who needs a good listener.
- Let someone cry on your shoulder.
- Include a single person in your family activities and holidays.
- Give a single mom or dad the day off.
- Acknowledge the birthday of someone who would otherwise be forgotten.
- Tell a funny joke to someone who could use a good laugh.
- If a friend is going through a rough time, pay to have her hair and nails done or anonymously send her a few dollars, or both, if you're able.
- Mail a handwritten letter to your child(ren), not an email.
- Sit and talk with a senior citizen.

- Mail a handwritten letter of love and encouragement to your spouse.
- Make a date with your spouse at a specified time each week.
- Make a date separately with each of your children at a specified time each week.
- Pay a surprise visit to someone who would just love to see you.
- Let someone know you're praying for them today — and then do it!

Reaching out to others, particularly those from whom you stand nothing to gain, will bring a special joy to your own heart. A shift in focus away from your own circumstances is what will enable you.

BE A FRIEND

Every one that comes into your life is there for a reason. Some may come quickly and leave just as quickly. You may never know why. Others, for some reason, become fast friends and stay for a while or longer, forever leaving the loving impressions you feel whenever the thought of them crosses your heart.

I've heard people say,

"AS LONG AS YOU HAVE A FRIEND, YOU'LL NEVER BE POOR."

I'm certain that's true. And, if at the time of your death you are able to count the number of *true* friends on one hand, you are rich beyond measure and extraordinarily blessed. To have even one ranks right up there with the greatest blessing possible. To be one is a testimony to the greatest of character.

These days, the word *friend* is hardly a coveted title anymore often ascribed to even the most casual of associates. The word is so carelessly tossed about that its true meaning has practically evaporated. In many cases, the so-called friends you know can be described as the "fair weather" type available only when it's to their advantage to be so, but quick to beat a hasty retreat when your luck goes south and they suspect you might really need them.

Webster's Dictionary defines "friend" in the following ways:

1. intimate associate or confidante,
2. loyal supporter,
3. somebody one knows and likes; and,
4. someone who will help/sacrifice.

Do any of those definitions describe you?

Christ set the best example for what it means to be a friend through the relationship He had with His disciples while here on earth.

"GREATER LOVE HAS NO MAN THAN THIS, THAT HE LAY DOWN HIS LIFE FOR HIS FRIENDS." JOHN 15:13

No, we may not have to literally die for our friends, but there are other ways we can help those in need. When they're hurting, we can offer a word of comfort

(Proverbs 12:15). If they're lonely or confused, we can listen. Sometimes just being there is all that's needed for someone to know you care. In times of trouble, a friend won't ask "Why?" only "What can I do to help?"

Is there someone you can think of who needs a friend right now? Sometimes just seeing your face is enough to make someone's day. Do whatever you can do to be the kind of friend you would want someone to be to you. Surprise others sometimes with spontaneous expressions of the love and appreciation you have for them while you still have the chance. You'll have no regrets and the Lord will be highly pleased.

**So, go 'head — make someone else's day
. . . and make yours in the process!**

Write down for the coming generation what the Lord did, so that people not yet born will praise Him.

Psalms 102:18

What I Want on My Tombstone

My Legacy

I want my life to be one that counts for Jesus; to be a help to others and to leave them some how better for having known me. I want to inspire others through my character and example: to do more and to be more, and to look towards Heaven for faith and strength to accomplish worthy goals.

I want to enjoy peace and harmony with others and am willing to do whatever is necessary to have it. I want people I love to *know* that I love them by the way I've actively treated them, and that there not be one person able to say truthfully in their heart that I ever did anything intentionally or maliciously to bring harm to them. I want the people I love to be provided for and protected.

I want to be genuinely and affectionately remembered in the hearts of a few when I'm gone based on how much I've loved them, not by any material accomplishments

I want to inspire my children, Beverly and Darnley, to develop and strengthen their own walk with the Lord through a personal relationship with Him while they're still young and viable, able to be used mightily by the Lord within the parameters of His plan for their lives and their future.

ABOUT THE AUTHOR

MARGARET-ANN BOGERTY is the consummate big sister. A few moments spent with her and you'll easily see why she's often described as "your best friend."

For almost 20 years, she has enjoyed success as a sales and marketing professional while concurrently an Adjunct Professor in the Schools of Business at Strayer University, George Mason University and the University of the District of Columbia. She has an M.B.A. degree from the University of New Haven in West Haven, Connecticut, and has been a motivational speaker featured frequently on the national circuit of Clemson University's Professional Development for Women Conferences.

Margaret-Ann is the very proud mother of Beverly and Darnley, two of the finest young people on earth. They live in Alexandria, Virginia, across the Potomac River from the nation's capitol. She enjoys rollerblading and she makes the best chocolate cake on earth!

Margaret-Ann is available for training workshops, seminars, and speaking forums everywhere. To schedule an engagement, contact her at

(powermrktg@aol.com)
www.greatparkingspace.com

Give the Gift of *I Always Get a Great Parking Space!*
To Your Friends and Colleagues
Check Your Local Bookstore or Order Here

☐ YES, I want_____copies of *I Always Get a Great Parking Space!*
for $13.95.

☐ YES, I am interested in having Margaret-Ann Bogerty speak or give
a seminar at my church, business, school, or organization. Please
send information.

Include $3.00 shipping and handling per book. Include applicable sales tax.
US funds only.

Payment must accompany orders.

Allow 4 - 6 weeks for delivery

My check or money order for $_____ is enclosed.

Name _____

Organization _____

Address _____

City/State/Zip _____

Phone (   )_____E-mail_____

___VISA ___MC ___AMEX ___DISC Card#_____

Signature_____ Exp. Date_____/_____

Make checks or money orders payable & retun to:
Power Marketing Publishing
P.O. Box 15631
Alexandria, Va 22309-1844
(703) 780-2745
powermrktg@aol.com